D&S
Vol. 10
Production Version
Part 1

B-29 Superfortress

in detail & scale

Alwyn T. Lloyd

Aero Publishers, Inc. U.S.A.

Arms and Armour Press London - Melbourne

This book is a product of Detail & Scale, Inc. which has sole responsibility for the contents and layout. Published and distributed in the United States by Aero Publishers, Inc., and in London and Melbourne by Arms & Armour Press.

CONTRIBUTORS:

Dana Bell
Steve Birdsall
Peter M. Bowers
Walter J. Boyne
Lonna Brooks
Sean Day
Ken DeJarlais
Harry S. Gann
Chuck Hansen
Joseph Harlick
Roger Harney
Gerald Hasselwander
Lloyd S. Jones
Herbert L. Lamb
Rob Mack
Hanna Massie
Clyde Matteson
David W. Menard
Monogram Models, Inc.
Marilyn A. Phipps
Don Price
Revell, Inc.
D.Q. Roberts
Victor D. Seely
Z. Joe Thornton
Guy M. Townsend
Gene Vik
Vivian White
Jack Wecker
Byron L. Wyngett
Sherman W. Wilkins
Gordon S. Williams

Bert Kinzey

The Boeing Company Historical Services and Public Relations Departments
AFLC Historian, Wright-Patterson AFB
Alfred F. Simpson Historical Research Center, Maxwell AFB
1361st Audio-Visual Squadron (MAC), NAS Anacostia
USAF Museum, Wright-Patterson AFB
National Air and Space Museum, Washington, D.C.

Published in United States by

Aero Publishers, Inc.
329 W. Aviation Road
Fallbrook, CA 92028

Published in Great Britain by

Arms and Armour Press
Lionel Leventhal Limited
2-6 Hampstead High Street
London NW3 1QQ
and in Australasia at
4-12 Tattersalls Lane
Melbourne, Victoria 3000

Library of Congress Cataloging in Publication Data

Lloyd, Alwyn T.
B-29 Superfortress in Detail & Scale.

(D & S; v. 10)
Contents: pt. 1. Production version.
1. B-29 bomber. I. Title.
UG 1242.B6L565 1983 358.4'2
83-2789
ISBN 0-8168-5019-4 (pbk. : pt. 1)

British Library Cataloging in Publication Data:

Lloyd, Alwyn T.
B-29 Superfortress in Detail and Scale.
(Detail and Scale series)
Part 1
1. B-29 bomber
I. Title II. Series
623.74'63 UG1264.B6
ISBN 0-85368-527-4

Printed and Published in the USA by Aero Publishers, Inc.

Front Cover: Renton - built B-29A, 42-93869. (Boeing K252)

Rear Cover: Tail view reveals the .50 caliber machine guns, 20 mm cannon, tail gunner's position, formation light, and rudder hinge detail. (Boeing K266)

INTRODUCTION

In this staged exploded view, the various major subassemblies of the B-29 are clearly visible.
(Boeing BW-24041)

Most historians will probably agree that the B-17 Flying Fortress was the most important allied heavy bomber of World War II. It was in the war from beginning to end, it served in all theaters, and it certainly was the best known bomber used by any nation during that war. But the B-29 was equally as important. While it was not used until comparatively late in the war, and although it was only used in the Pacific against Japan, its influence on the outcome of the war was as dramatic as it was different when compared to the B-17.

The B-29 was a giant step forward in technology over every bomber before it. It had pressurized compartments, remotely aimed defensive armament, and many other new features. Bombing tactics used with the B-17s over Germany had to be changed for the B-29, and the B-29, with its AN/APQ-13 and Eagle radars, ushered in the first widespread use of radar and "blind" bombing.

But the biggest influence the B-29 had on history was felt on two missions in August 1945. The B-29 became the first bomber to use a nuclear weapon in combat. By dropping two atomic bombs on Japan, the B-29 eliminated the need for an invasion of the Japanese homeland, and thereby saved many hundreds of thousands of lives on both sides that would have been lost if such an invasion had taken place. Hopefully, history will record that the B-29 will be the only bomber ever to use a nuclear weapon.

It is also interesting to note that the B-29 had quite an influence on the Soviet Union. After World War II the Soviet aircraft design bureau Tupolev produced an exact copy of the B-29 which was designated the Tu-4. It was codenamed "Bull" by NATO.

Al Lloyd has followed his first B-17 book with this volume on the B-29. Again he has been able to use many photos that have never before been released, and has shown the B-29 in more detail than ever possible before. As part 1, this book covers the production versions of the Superfortress, and later, part 2 will cover the SB rescue, KB tanker, F-9 and RB-29 recon versions, and the nuclear bombers in detail.

Detail & Scale and Aero Publishers are pleased to present the most detailed coverage of the B-29 ever released in a single publication.

The Model 341 was the initial Boeing design concept for the Army Air Corps' super bomber program. (Boeing HS 1608)

DEVELOPMENTAL HISTORY

In November 1939, the U.S. Army Air Corps developed a concept for a super bomber which would fly at speeds of 400 miles per hour, have a 5,333-mile range, and carry a one-ton bomb load over half that distance. These specifications were sent to four aircraft manufacturers on 29 January 1940. Response from these manufacturers resulted in the following Air Corps mission-design sequence designations: B-29 (Boeing Model 345), B-30 (Lockheed Model 51-81-01), B-31 (Douglas Model 332F), and B-32 (Consolidated Model 33). The B-30 was based on the C-69 Constellation and the B-31 was derived from the XB-19. Neither the B-30 nor the B-31 would leave the drawing boards.

Boeing had already initiated preliminary design studies in June 1938, and the Boeing Model 341 design was submitted to the Air Corps on 11 March 1940. Revisions to this submittal resulted in the Model 345. Even before the first flight of the B-29, Boeing was awarded a contract for 14 YB-29s and 250 B-29s which would be built at a new government owned factory in Wichita, Kansas.

On 6 September 1940, the Army Air Forces let a contract for the first two XB-29s. A contract for the service evaluation YB-29s and production B-29s was issued on 10 June 1941. The first flight of the XB-29 was made from Boeing Field in Seattle, Washington, on 21 September 1942. Production airplanes were initially delivered on 29 June 1943 and received operational status in September of the same year.

A basic problem confronting the Boeing designers was how to propel a mass more than twice the weight of a B-17 at a speed that was more than twice that of a Flying Fortress. On the surface this appears to be a simple problem -- double the speed of the airplane by doubling the size of the engines. Aerodynamically this is not possible. In rough numbers, the horsepower requirement goes up as the cube of the velocity. Therefore, twice the speed requires eight times the horsepower. Then account for the doubled weight and the induced drag on the airplane again goes up, thus requiring even greater horsepower. The B-17s were powered by four R-1820 engines developing 1,200 horsepower; or a total of 4,800 horsepower. The

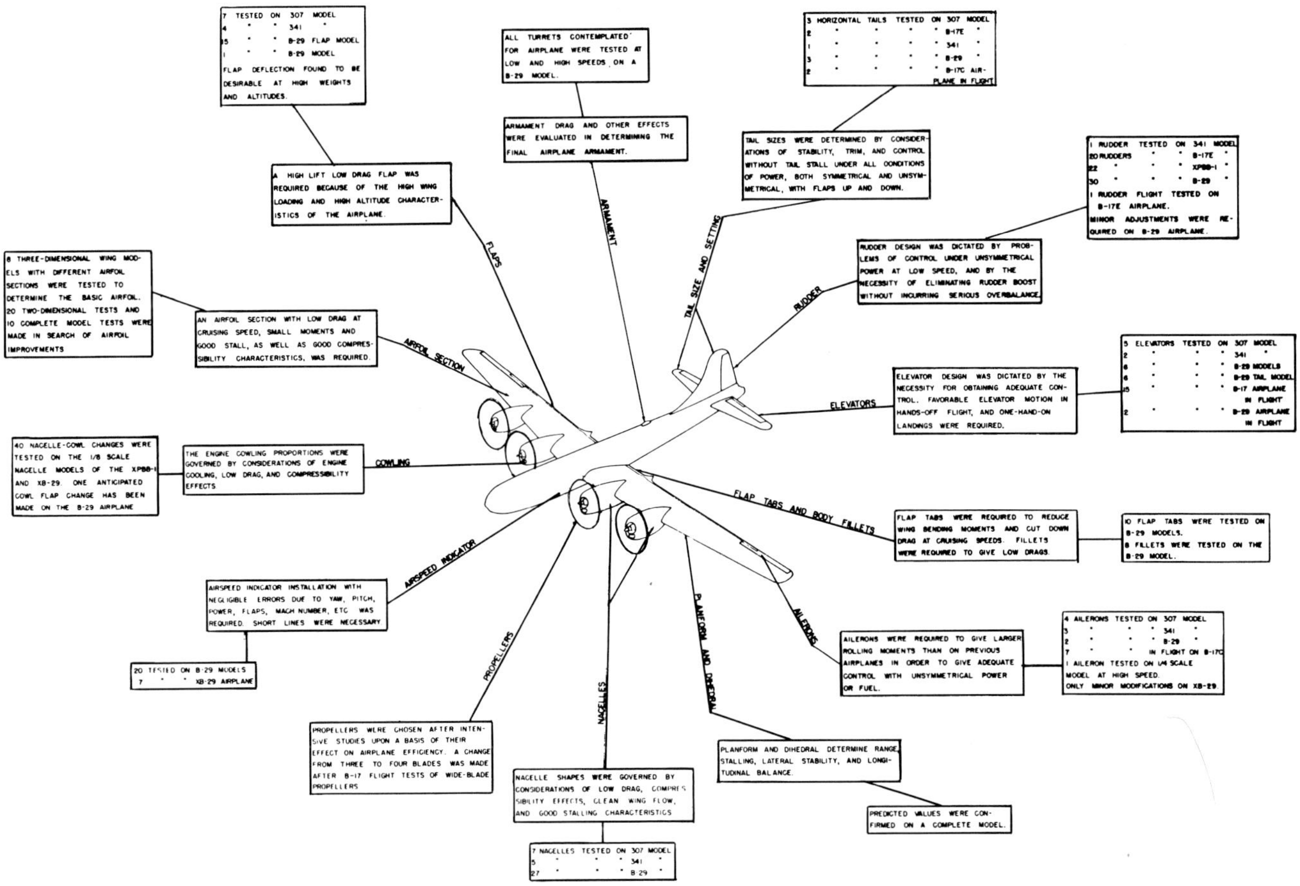

B-29 AERODYNAMIC DEVELOPMENT

18-cylinder Wright Cyclone R-3350 engine, originally used on the XB-19, developed 2,200 horsepower and was the largest available powerplant. Four R-3350s developing 8,800 horsepower would be woefully inadequate to power the B-29. To resolve this dilema, Boeing set out to minimize the drag on the airframe.

Thirteen major areas of concern were exercised through engineering analysis, wind tunnel tests, and flight testing. A summary of these design pursuits appears in the figure shown above. The results of Boeing's design efforts was an unusual (for that day) combination of flight and landing characteristics which compromised neither. The sleek aerodynamic design performed well in flight. Fowler flaps were added to the high-speed wings to reduce the speed for takeoff and landing.

The greatest problems experienced with the B-29 Superfortress centered around the early R-3350 engines which were difficult to cool. These cooling problems resulted in internal engine failures and induction system fires. One of the XB-29s crashed due to an engine fire, killing the entire crew. Changes to the cowl flaps, a revised collector ring installation, and valve cooling helped relieve the engine overheating problems. Revisions to the cowling and engine ducting reduced the potential for backfiring and induction system fires.

One of the greatest tributes to the B-29 was given by General Henry H. "Hap" Arnold when he summed up the story of the war with Japan. He stated that the Japanese surrender was not entirely due to the result of the two atomic bomb attacks. In other raids the B-29 hit some 60 Japanese cities with regular high explosive and incendiary bombs. The B-29s had destroyed most of the Japanese industries. Mine-laying B-29s prevented the arrival of incoming cargos of critical items. As a result, the enemy was unable to carry on a large-scale war. Many Japanese leaders gave credit to the B-29 attacks on their mainland interior and industrial cities as the greatest single factor in forcing their surrender. Some Japanese went so far as to say that the B-29 reduced their military production by as much as 50 percent. The manhours, money and trust invested in the B-29 Superfortress by the U.S. Army Air Forces was justified by its success.

With full war paint this view of the XB-19 shows the nose and forward top turrets with a .50 caliber machine gun and a 37 mm cannon in each location. The aft top turret has been removed. (AFM 0-215)

For a time both the B-29 and B-32 utilized the same vertical fin and rudder. The horizontal tail remained essentially the same on both aircraft. The aircraft depicted in this photograph is the first B-32-1-CF. (AFM 150332)

Two other aircraft had considerable influence on the B-29. First was the Douglas XB-19 which used the Wright R-3350 engines. The engines proved troublesome for the XB-19 as they would later for the B-29. But the data obtained from testing the R-3350 on the XB-19 had a direct bearing on the future use of these engines on the B-29 and the B-32 and C-69/C-121 as well.

The second aircraft to be closely related to the B-29 from the developmental standpoint was the Consolidated Vultee B-32 Dominator. It was developed as an insurance package for the USAAF "Superbomber" project in the event the B-29 did not meet its required performance guarantees. While much of the B-24 Liberator design was incorporated into the B-32, it also had features in common with the B-29. For a while, the vertical tail surfaces were the same, but the tail on the B-32 was later changed. The horizontal tails on the two aircraft were essentially the same, and both aircraft utilized the Wright R-3350 engines.

CONTEMPORARY FOUR-ENGINED BOMBER COMPARISONS

Manufacturer/ Type	No. Built (All Models)	Span	Length	Height	Empty Wt. (Pounds)	Gross Wt. (Pounds)	Service Ceiling	Cruise/Top Speed (MPH)	Engines	H.P.	Range	Bomb Load
Boeing XB-15	1	149′	87′7″	18′1″	-	70,706	18,900′	152/200	P&W "Twin Wasp"	850	5,130	8,000
Boeing B-17G	12,731	103′9″	74′4″	19′1″	36,135	55,000	35,600′	160/302	Wright R-1820-97	1,200	3,400	8,000
Douglas XB-19	1	212′	132′4″	34′	84,431	140,000	39,000′	135/224	Wright R-3350-5	2,000	7,710	16,000
Consolidated B-24J	18,842	110′	67′2″	18′	36,500	56,000	28,000′	215/290	P&W R-1830-65	1,200	3,700	8,800
Boeing B-29	3,654 *	141′3″	99′	27′9″	70,140	110,000	31,850′	220/365	Wright R-3350-23	2,200	5,830	20,000
Boeing/Bell B-29B	311	141′3″	99′	27′8″	68,821	135,744	38,100′	344/354	Wright R-3350-57 R-3350-57A	2,200	6,023	10,000
Consolidated B-32	115	135′	82′1″	32′2″	60,278	100,000	29,600′	290/357	Wright R-3350-23	2,200	4,200	8,000

* Includes B-29s other than B-29Bs.

XB-29

The first XB-29 without turrets. The rudder extends down into the area later to be occupied by the tail gunner's position. A large fixed tail bumper is visible. Note the early placement of the dual pitot probes on top of the vertical fin. An early experimental sighting blister is visible just forward of the national insignia.

(Boeing P32040)

Three flyable XB-29s and a static test article were ordered by the Army Air Corps. Serial number 41-002 was the first B-29 to fly, and it served as a test bed throughout the war. The second aircraft, S/N 41-003, experienced an uncontrollable engine fire on takeoff from Boeing Field on 18 February 1943. The aircraft crashed into the Frye & Company meat packing plant as the crew desperately attempted to return to the field. Killed in the crash was Boeing's veteran test pilot Eddie Allen and ten other crewmen, including some of the cream of the crop of young University of Washington graduates hired for the war effort. The third XB-29 was S/N 41-18335.

Initial flight testing of the XB-29s was made without armament. Four R-3350-13 engines turned 17-foot diameter three-bladed Hamilton Standard hydromatic propellers. A commander's dome was prominently mounted aft of the cockpit, and dual pitot probes were installed on top of the vertical stabilizer. Initially the rudder came to the base of the fin into the area later to be occupied by the tail gunner's station.

After a short while of operation, the Boeing crews decided to name the first aircraft The Flying Guinea Pig. The flight test personnel were then in search of an artist -- a commodity hard to find in those years. Finally they located a riveter in the shops who had been a sign painter and asked him to paint the airplane. He was shown a dictionary with a sketch of a guinea pig and asked to make it into a flying guinea pig. A sketch was made, complete with grid lines. The drawing was then enlarged and placed on both sides of the aircraft. The watch, with hands set at 4 o'clock was added because the airplane had a reputation of not being airworthy until after that hour.

The third XB-29-BO, S/N 41-18335 displays its three-bladed propellers, commander's dome, and fin-mounted pitot probes. The fabric control surfaces have been painted in standard camouflage colors.

(Boeing-Wichita 282-156)

The Flying Guinea Pig lifts off from Boeing Field. Note that the fin-mounted pitot probes have been deleted. (D.C. Whitworth)

Run up with the Curtiss electric propellers. (Boeing P6702)

The prototype XB-29 on a muddy Boeing Field apron. Originally the aircraft was fitted with three-bladed propellers. A commander's dome may be seen immediately ahead of the forward upper turret.(Boeing FA948 (via D.C. Whitworth)

At this point in her life the prototype XB-29 has Curtiss electric propellers installed. The standard No. 2 cowl has been replaced by the experimental "Andy Gump" cowl -- a name derived from its old-man-like recessed chin scoop. ***(D.C. Whitworth)***

The original artwork for The Flying Guinea Pig nose art. ***(D.C. Whitworth)***

Nose art on the right side of the XB-29 clearly shows the watch reading 4 o'clock. ***(D.C. Whitworth)***

In this nose close-up, the pitot probes can now be seen located aft of the nose art. Note the nose wheel hub cap with the aircraft's secondary name "Moses Lake Belle" in honor of her alternate flight test home in eastern Washington. ***(D. C. Whitworth)***

XB-29 THREE VIEW DRAWING

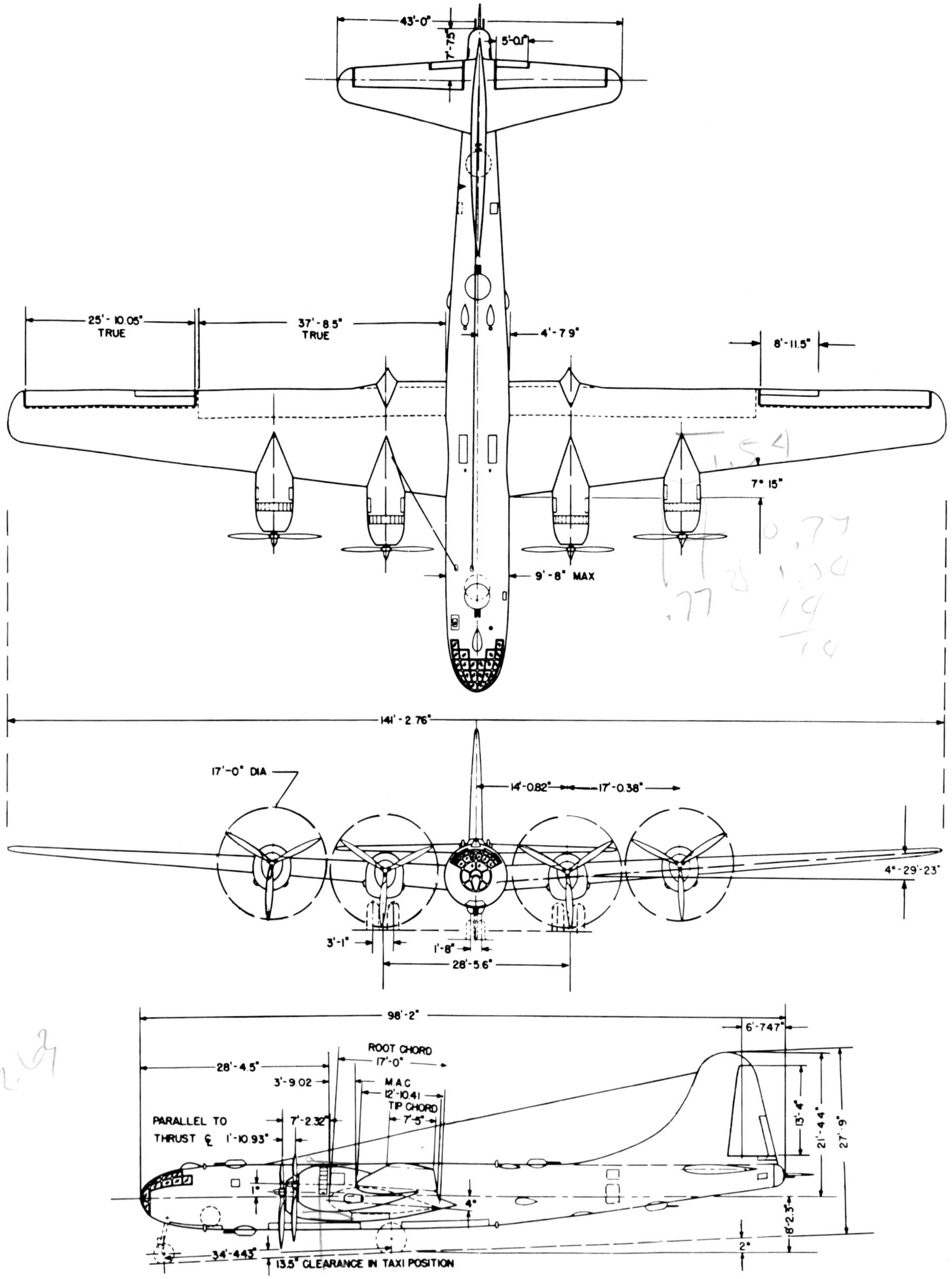

YB-29

Weighing the first YB-29-BW on 6 June 1943. The cowls and nacelles were yet to be painted. An astrodome was not installed on the YB-29s. ***(Boeing 62450/BW11392)***

The first production article B-29s were built at the Boeing-Wichita plant. A contract signed in June 1941 provided for production of 14 YB-29s at a unit cost of $1,403,623.86. Supplements to this contract, W535 AC-19673, were written for all subsequent Boeing-Wichita B-29 production.

The 14 YB-29s were procurred for use as service test aircraft, and a full General Electric armament system was installed on the aircraft. Four R-3350-21 engines drove the three-bladed Hamilton Standard propellers. These aircraft were delivered with camouflage paint, and because of their delivery time frame, the national insignia covered the full spectrum of blue circle and white star, star and bar with red surrounds, and the star and bar with blue surround.

These aircraft were thrown into the "Battle of Kansas" in order to work out the bugs, being used as testbeds, trainers, and mock ups. Numerous accounts of their unusual use have been written.

YB-29-BW, S/N 41-36958, served as a trainer with the 444th Bomb Group prior to going to Seattle for use in the Boeing Fortress School. S/N 41-36960 once was dispatched to Marietta, GA, where it was towed around the ramps while fully loaded to determine if a 120,000-pound airframe would damage the paving. After testing as a YB-29, S/N 41-36954 was sent to General Motors for installation of 24 cylinder Allison V-3420-11 liquid-cooled engines and was redesignated the XB-39. Another YB-29 was outfitted to carry an additional 10 machine guns, giving it a total of 20, so that it could be used as a bomber escort. In January 1944, YB-29, S/N 42-36964, was allocated to Tinker Field, OK, for mock up requirements necessary for the XX Bomber Command operations.

As a ploy, YB-29, S/N 42-36963, was flown from Kansas to Miami. Under secret orders the aircraft made a night takeoff and flew south over the Atlantic, then headed north to Gander Field, Newfoundland. From there it made a non-stop flight at 24,000 feet to England. Within 45 minutes of its arrival, a high-flying Luftwaffe reconnaissance plane photographed the YB-29. It remained in England for two weeks where it was inspected by Allied leaders. Information leaks were made about the aircraft not meeting expectations for use as a bomber in the Pacific war and that it might be relegated to an armed transport role. This aircraft then flew to Kharagpur, India, arriving on 6 April 1944. It was the second B-29 in the theater and the only YB-29 to serve in combat. Named Hobo Queen, she was assigned to the 462nd BG and was used as a tanker to ferry fuel over the Hump.

In February 1944, the Air Proving Ground Command at Eglin Field, FL, conducted armament tests on a YB-29 fitted with the General Electric fire control system having manned turrets. Martin upper turrets, Bell nose and tail mounts, Sperry retractable lower ball turrets, and hand held guns in the waist comprised the system. Though more effective, these manual turrets were in unpressurized areas thereby negating the high altitude crew comfort of the pressurized aircraft. The reason that the B-29s were able to defend themselves so well in combat was more because of the inherent superiority of the aircraft than the armament.

The third YB-29 is being towed to be painted. The first two camouflaged YB-29s appear in the background.
(Boeing 62689/BW11901)

The No. 3 YB-29 being towed for painting. Note that the fabric control surfaces have already been painted. Control surfaces are painted and balanced prior to installation on the aircraft to ensure their flight characteristics.
(Boeing 62688/BW11900)

The seventh YB-29 in flight. The de-icer boots have been removed. The APU hatch may be discerned adjacent to the forward edge of the vertical fin. *(Boeing BW15751)*

Right: No. 2 power package on a YB-29. The propeller is a 3-bladed Hamilton Standard hydromatic. Cowl flaps are open. The exhaust stack is located just forward of the main wheel well.
(Boeing 62511/BW11555)

Below: No. 1 engine on a YB-29. Access panels for the superchargers have been removed. Note the red surround on the national insignia.
(Boeing 63045/BW12706)

THE B-29 DESCRIBED

A B-29-90-BW with the four-gun top front turret, two mast antennas on the fuselage top, and sporting a black under-belly. The high-stress upper wing surface panels are clearly shown in this view. (Boeing photo)

The basic appearance of the B-29 was unchanged throughout its production life. Many of the components were interchangeable between all variants of the aircraft.

Structure:

Lessons learned on the Model 299, B-17 Flying Fortress, and the Model 307 Stratoliner were employed in the structural design of the Model 345, B-29 Superfortress. The basic airframe was made from aluminum alloy formed into a semi-monocoque structure.

Fuselage:

A circular cross-section was employed in the fuselage design in order to afford maximum strength for pressurization and to minimize aerodynamic drag. The bulkheads, frames, and stringers were covered by a flush-riveted, butt-joined skin. Brazier head rivets were used only in the gun blast areas. Five sections comprised the fuselage. Three pressurized crew compartments were built into the airframe -- a forward, aft, and tail gunner's compartment. A 34-inch diameter, 33-foot long pressurized communication tunnel connected the forward and aft crew compartments. Access to the tail gunner's position was through the unpressurized aft fuselage.

Wing:

The new Boeing 117 airfoil was designed for the B-29. This airfoil was a prime factor in overall drag reduction, being extremely efficient through its 11.5 aspect ratio. The aircraft was inherently stable through use of a 4.5-degree dihedral angle and a 7-degree leading edge sweepback. Should the airplane fall off on one wing in a stall, the airplane would immediately bank then assume a steep glide straight forward. At maximum gross weight the wing loading was 69 pounds per square foot -- a figure the USAAF tried to reduce.

To achieve a landing speed equal to that of the B-17, large Fowler flaps were used. These track-mounted flaps extended downward and aft, thereby increasing the wing area and the downwash angle of the air leaving the wing. A 19% increase in overall wing area was achieved when these flaps were fully extended.

A line up of B-29-60-BWs on the Wichita factory ramp. The four-gun top front turret is apparent. Behind the turret is the navigator's astrodome. (Boeing BW22148)

Basically the wing was made up of five sections. Each section was essentially a torque box made up of a front and rear spar connected by ribs. Web ribs replaced the bolted tubing ribs used on the B-17. Nose and trailing edge ribs afforded the requisite airfoil sections for the wing, and flush-riveted, butt-jointed skins were installed over the basic wing structure. On most B-29s the two-wing center section halves were built onto the inboard wing panels for insertion into the fuselage. The Renton-built B-29As had a single-piece center section stub built into the fuselage with a resultant 1-foot increase in span. The inboard wing panels embodied the nacelles, flaps, and landing gear. The outboard panels, containing the fabric-covered ailerons, were joined at Wing Station 510.

Empennage:

The tail surfaces on the B-29 were developed from those on the B-17. They consisted of cantilevered vertical and horizontal stabilizers comprised of spars and ribs covered with stressed sheet metal skins. Fabric was employed on the rudder and elevators.

Flight Controls:

All of the primary flight controls (ailerons, rudder, and elevators) were cable-operated. Redundant systems were employed to reduce the hazard of combat damage. All secondary flight controls were electrically operated.

Hydraulic System:

Combat experience showed that electrical systems were less vulnerable to enemy fire than hydraulic systems. As a consequence the brakes were the only hydraulically-operated system on the airplane.

Electrical System:

The 28-volt direct current was supplied by six engine-driven generators which turned at 2.8 times the engine crankshaft speed. A pair of generators were installed on engines No. 1 and 4, while single generators were mounted on engines No. 2 and 3. The P-2 type generators were rated at 200 amperes at 5,000 to 10,000 rpm. A similar generator was also mounted on the auxiliary power unit (APU) located in the unpressurized aft fuselage. APU power was used for engine starting and emergency power. The B-29 APU was either a horizontally opposed Lawrence Model 20A, or an Andover 90-degree V-type air-cooled gasoline engine. Both APUs were of the 2-cylinder, 4-cycle type. A single 34-ampere/hour 24-volt battery, located forward of the APU, served to stabilize the voltage in the D.C. buses.

Alternating current was provided by a pair of inverters which converted the 24-volt D.C. to 26-volt and 115-volt, 400-cycle A.C. power. This electrical system powered the autotsyn instruments, radio compass, electronic turbo-regulator, and flux-gate compass.

Fuel System:

For maximum reliability, each engine had an individual fuel system -- direct tank-to-engine fuel supply. Each system was comprised of a self-sealing fuel tank, an electrically-driven boost pump, a solenoid-operated fuel shut-off valve, a fuel strainer, an engine-driven fuel pump, and a hydrometering pressure type carburetor.

Four main fuel tanks were located in the inboard wing between the spars. The inboard tanks were divided into four cells and supplied the inboard engines. The outboard tanks were divided into seven cells and supplied the outboard engines. In the event of battle damage or equipment malfunction, fuel could be transferred from one tank to another. Fuel from an intact tank could be transferred into a damaged tank to permit fuel feed to its respective engine.

Additional fuel could be carried in four releasable auxiliary fuel tanks mounted in the bomb bays. Two tanks could be installed in each bay. The Goodyear 2FI-6-4562 self-sealing tanks were supported internally by fiber hoops. B-7 bomb shackles and A-2 bomb releases were used to attach the tanks to the 500-pound bomb racks.

All fuel cells were constructed of layers of buna-N covered fabric, compound rubber sealant, rayon, and nylon. Wooden hoops were used to give rigidity to the wing tank fuel cells.

(Note: Fuel system details are shown on page 41.)

Pitot Static System:

A pair of G-2 pitot probes and a set of 9/32-inch

diameter holes comprised the pitot static system pick-up points. The pitot masts were located on each side of the forward pressurized compartment at Station 109. The static ports were located along the horizontal centerline of the aircraft -- the left source was directly beneath the navigator's window, while the right source was located directly opposite.

Landing Gear:

The major components of the B-29 landing gear system were the dual nose wheel, the dual main wheels, and the tail skid. The main wheels and tires were interchangeable with those on the B-17F, B-17G, and the B-24 aircraft. The 16-ply, 56-inch diameter main gear tires had a nylon cord casing and puncture-proof inner tubes. Under normal conditions, 100-150 landings could be made with a good tire. The nose gear had 10-ply, nylon cord, smooth contour, 36-inch diameter tires.

The tail skid was located between body stations 1039-1076 and served to protect the lower rear turret during takeoffs and landings.

All of the landing gear system components were electrically operated and required approximately one minute to raise the gear. The emergency extension systems were also electrical. A manual retraction system was added with B-29-45-BW, B-29A-15-BN, B-29-30-BA, and B-29-20-MO. (Note: Landing gear details are shown on pages 44 and 45.)

Crew Life Support:

Normally the cabin supercharging and heating system was used to afford crew comfort when the aircraft was operated above 10,000 feet, and a 10,000-foot cabin environment could be maintained up to 30,000 feet. Procedures called for progressive manual release of cabin pressure 30 minutes prior to entering a combat zone. The cabin was unpressurized during combat in order to preclude a rapid decompression should the aircraft sustain battle damage.

Crew oxygen was used during unpressurized flight above 10,000 feet. Each crewman was supplied by an A-12 oxygen demand regulation located at each crew station. To provide for crew mobility, a number of A-4 portable oxygen units were carried on board. The walk-around bottles allowed 6-12 minutes of operation before they had to be recharged at one of the refill valves located at each crew station.

Communications and Navigation Equipment:

A number of standard pieces of electronic gear were carried on the B-29 for communications and navigation. The equipment carried for air-to-air, air-to-ground, and interplane communication consisted of: SCR-274-N command set, SCR-287 liaison set, SCR-211 frequency meter, RC-36 interphone equipment, and RC-198 filter equipment. For navigation, the aircraft carried: SCR-269G radio compass and a RC-43A marker beacon. An RC-103 blind landing system was installed, the SCR-578 emergency sea rescue dinghy transmitter was carried, and lastly, the SCR-695 IFF radio was on board.

The AN/APQ-13 airborne radar system was used on the B-29 and B-29A for navigation and high altitude bombing. These aircraft also carried the AN/APQ-4 airborne navigational equipment to determine the geographic position of the aircraft.

The B-29Bs had a completely different radar system. An AN/APQ-7 Eagle radar system was employed for both navigation and bombing. The Eagle radar could be identified by its 18-foot airfoil wing antenna located between the bomb bays. Further, these aircraft had the AN/APG-15B airborne radar gun sighting system in the tail of the aircraft for night protection from enemy fighters. (Note: Details of the communications system are shown on page 41.)

Powerplant:

The 18-cylinder Wright Cyclone R-3350-5 engine was originally used on the Douglas XB-19, and was subsequently developed for the B-29. Fuel with a 100-octane rating was used in this powerplant. The engine was comprised of four sections: nose, power, supercharger, and accessory.

The nose section contained a planetary-type reduction gear which reduced the propeller shaft rpm to .35 that of the crankshaft speed. A propeller governor was mounted on top of the nose section.

The power section was comprised of two staggered rows of nine cylinders each. Cooling fins were integrally cast into the aluminum alloy cylinder heads, and were also located on the steel cylinder barrels. R-3350-13 and -21 engines had these fins machined into the cylinder barrels, while the R-3350-23 engines were known as "combat engines," and had aluminum alloy fins pressed into the barrels. The front cylinders exhausted forward into the front collector ring, while the rear cylinders exhausted into the rear collector ring. The front collector ring sections directed the exhaust through flexible couplings into the rear collector ring. The exhaust was then directed to the exhaust transition ducts on each side of the engine. Then the exhaust passed through the left or right supercharger turbine wheels before exiting the flight hoods on each side of the nacelle.

In the supercharging section, a pair of General Electric B-11 exhaust-driven turbo-superchargers enabled the engines to maintain sea level horsepower up to 33,000 feet. Each unit consisted of a single-speed blower with a 6.06-to-1 impeller-to-crankshaft gear ratio. This supercharged induction air was then directed through a Chandler-Evans Type 58 CPB-4 pressure carburetor mounted on top of the supercharger. This system could maintain a pressurized fuel-air mixture at approximately 17 inches of mercury at 2,400 rpm.

In the accessory section, a series of gear trains operated the fuel pump, generators, vacuum pump, oil pumps, starter, and hydraulic pump.

The cowlings were comprised of a fixed cowl ring, a set of side panels, and ten moveable cowl flaps. On early engines, the propeller, cowl ring, and side panels had to be removed in order to change the 36 spark plugs. Later cowls were manufactured with removeable side panels -- a feature which was also retrofitted. An electric motor in each nacelle operated the cowl flaps by means of flexible drive shafts interconnecting individual jackscrews for each flap. (Note: Engine details are shown on pages 46 and 47.)

Propellers:

Basic B-29s had Hamilton Standard hydromatic, constant speed propellers. Both the XB-29s and YB-29s had 3-bladed, 17-foot diameter propellers. Production B-29s were equipped with 4-bladed, 16'7" diameter, full-feathering propellers. The latter propellers operated at 7/20th the speed of the engine crankshaft with resultant low tip speeds, higher propeller efficiency, and reduced noise. An isopropal alcohol anti-icing system was installed on the aircraft.

Curtiss electric propellers were installed on a number of B-29s, including the B-29Bs. These propellers were reversible and synchronized simultaneously with a single control.

Deicing Equipment:

A pulsating deicer boot system was installed on the leading edges of the wings, horizontal stabilizer, and vertical stabilizer. These boots were later eliminated because combat experience showed that they could be of more harm than good should they become damaged and interfere with the flight controls. In production the boots were eliminated with B-29-50-BW, B-29A-5-BN, B-29-20-BA, and B-29-20-MO. After World War II these boots re-appeared on "winterized" B-29s. Some B-29s used during the Korean "Police Action" were equipped with deicer boots.

Exterior Lighting:

As with most aircraft, the B-29 was equipped with the standard red (left), green (right), and white (tail) position lights.

Three blue formation lights were installed on top of each wing and a pair were located on top of the fuselage.

The identification lights consisted of a white light on top of the fuselage and three (red, green, and amber) lights located under the fuselage.

A bomb release formation light was used to signal airplanes following in formation that the bombs were being dropped while the formation was engaged in mass or pattern bombing. The white lamp was mounted in the fairing above the tail gunner's rear window. (Note: Lighting details are shown on page 42).

Cameras:

Three electrically-operated strike cameras were carried on the B-29. One vertical and two oblique cameras were installed forward of the lower rear turret in the unpressurized tail section. Basically the K-22, K-18, or K-7C cameras were carried.

In addition, various crew members had type K-20 hand-held, manually operated cameras. These cameras were capable of making up to 50 4 x 5 negatives on a single roll of film.

Offensive Armament:

The B-29 was equipped with a forward and aft bomb bay separated by the wing center section. Initially the bomb bay doors were electrically-actuated by motor-driven actuators installed at each end of the doors. While approaching the target, the doors were slowly opened, allowing the enemy plenty of time to assess the situation, and also increasing the drag for a longer period of time. Later, a pneumatic actuation system was incorporated with B-29-55-BW, B-29A-15-BN, B-29-30-BA, and B-29-25-MO. The pneumatic doors operated rapidly, and thereby reduced drag and enemy lead time. Unfortunately, these doors created a serious ground crew hazard, and a special tool (2 x 4 board) was used to hold the doors open during maintenance.

Proving Ground Command tests showed that pneumatic bomb bay doors operated satisfactorily when actuated by the bomb sight. When the doors were snapped open immediately prior to releasing the bombs, the B-29 was more stable on the bomb run since the vibration caused by the open bomb bay doors was eliminated. An emergency air system was recommended so as to ensure a complete cycle of door operation; thus preventing failure of the door to open or close if a cycle were left incompleted.

Three sizes of bomb racks were available for the B-29. A center rack could support 500 pounds of bombs. Interchangeable left and right hand racks

B-29 WALK-AROUND

Front view. The gentle 4.5° wing dihedral angle is apparent in this view. *(Boeing 64396/BW17063)*

Left front view. *(Boeing 64397/BW17062)*

Left side view. Superchargers are exposed. *(Boeing 64393/BW17058)*

Rear view. The horizontal tail is set at 90° to the vertical stabilizer. *(Boeing 64399/BW17064)*

Right rear view. *(Boeing 64394/BW17059)*

Right front view. *(Boeing 64395/BW17060)*

supported either 1000 or 4000 pounds of bombs. The 1000-pound racks could accommodate 100, 300, 500, or 1000-pound bombs. Bombs were carried on shackles which were attached to the bomb racks. The bomb racks served three functions: to carry bombs, to carry the auxiliary fuel tanks, or to carry a cargo platform. (Note: Offensive armament details are shown on pages 54, 55, and 56.)

Defensive Armament:

The B-29 was equipped with a General Electric Central Station Fire Control System. This defensive armament was comprised of a pair of upper and a pair of lower turrets and a tail turret. The tail turret was the only manned position. Primary control of both forward turrets was relegated to the bombardier. The side gunners shared primary control of the lower rear turret, while control of the upper rear turret was assigned to the central fire control (CFC) gunner. The CFC gunner also had secondary control of the upper forward turret. Secondary control of the lower forward turret and tail turret was shared by the two side gunners.

Originally the upper and lower turrets had pairs of .50 caliber machine guns installed. The 4-gun upper forward turret was introduced with B-29-40-BW, B-29A-20-BN, B-29-20-BA, and B-29-10-MO. These turrets were electrically-powered and controlled from the remote sighting stations. Initially each turret could hold 500 rounds of ammunition per gun in removeable magazine cans. Ammunition capacities were increased to 1000 rounds per gun with B-29-40-BW, B-29A-15-BN, B-29-20-BA, and B-29-10-MO. The quantity was then reduced back to 500 rounds per gun with B-29-60-BW, B-29-20-BA, and B-29-25-MO.

A contour follower and limit switch system precluded the remotely-sighted guns from firing into the airplane. To preclude interference with the nose gear doors, the lower forward turret had to be stowed in the aft position for takeoff and landing. Similarly, the lower rear turret had to be stowed in the aft position to preclude the guns from striking the ground. In addition, the lower forward guns had to be clear from the aft position to permit operation of the bomb bay doors.

Early B-29s had a tail turret equipped with a pair of .50 caliber machine guns and a 20 mm M-2 cannon. The .50 caliber ammunition was carried in a pair of large boxes located forward of the horizontal stabilizer at Body Station 1039.9. Tracks carried the ammunition aft to the tail guns. A total of 110 rounds were carried in the turret for the cannon. The cannon could be fired separately or in consort with the machine guns, but, because the cannon had a different trajectory than the machine guns, it was not effective. The cannon was deleted with B-29-55-BW, B-29A-20-BN, B-29-25-BA, and B-29-25-MO.

A 16 mm motion picture camera was located in each turret. The camera operated each time the guns were fired, and continued to operate for three seconds after firing.

Because of concern over heavy frontal fighter attack, and the poor reliability of the forward top two-gun turret, the Proving Ground Command tested a four-gun installation on a B-29. A standard P-61-style GE four-gun turret was modified by Emerson Electric Manufacturing Co. and installed in the upper forward and upper aft positions of a B-29. Modifications included the addition of a contour follower and more ammunition. Separate tests were conducted on each turret.

Test data for the forward turret indicated that pattern dispersion increased proportionally from the right outboard gun to the left outboard gun. Dispersion in the right guns was considered to be satisfactory, whereas it was unsatisfactory in the left guns. The increased dispersion toward the left was caused by torque in the gun mount which was the result of the elevation drive gear being located on the right side of the gun mount. It was recommended that a means be devised for stiffening the elevation mechanism to decrease the dispersion of the left outboard gun. It was believed that a four-gun turret was more desirable than a two-gun turret in the upper forward position because of the serious increase in nose vulnerability caused by a gun stoppage in the two-gun turret.

Test data for the aft top turret with a four-gun installation produced a similar dispersion pattern. Stiffening of the gun cradle was again suggested as a solution. Though the four-gun turret functioned satisfactorily in the aft top position, it was not as effective as the two-gun turret used in earlier tests. Therefore, it was recommended that the four-gun turret not be used in the upper aft position unless the large dispersion could be reduced.

The four-gun upper turret represented a considerable increase in weight and required more space than the two-gun turret. Contrary to expectations, the speed and climb performance of the B-29 with the four-gun turret were superior to those of the B-29 with the two-gun turret installed. Though unexplained, the Proving Ground Command did not believe that the superior performance was due to the type of turret used. (Note: Defensive armament details are shown on pages 57 thru 60.)

B-29A

The 20 mm cannon is visible just above the .50 caliber machine guns in this view of B-29A-5-BN, S/N 42-93869. The top front turret is missing from the aircraft due to a temporary production shortage. (Boeing X421)

Externally there was no visible difference between the B-29s built by Boeing-Wichita (BW), Bell-Marietta (BA), or Martin-Omaha (MO) and the Boeing-Renton (BN) B-29A. However, there was a major difference in the wing installation. The B-29A had a stub wing center section installed into the fuselage; whereas all other B-29s had a pair of inboard wing panels joined at the centerline of the aircraft. The B-29A span was increased by one foot. This difference alone was sufficient to warrant a new aircraft designator.

This structural change simplified construction, but had some adverse effects on the aircraft performance since the heavier structure increased the empty weight by 706 pounds. In addition, the useable fuel capacity was reduced by 213 gallons in the center wing tank (1333 vs. 1083 gallons total capacity).

Left: Close up of the nose on a B-29A. Windshield wipers are not installed on the pilots' windows. Defroster tubes for the upper part of the bombardier's nose piece are visible. Flakcurtains are installed on the lower windows of the bombardier's nose piece. Interior details of the cockpit are quite apparent in this view. (Boeing 96561-B)

Below: B-29A-40-BN in the flare to land at Boeing Field. Fowler flap with inboard nacelle tail cone is clearly visible. (G. S. Williams)

Flight line with B-29A-10-BNs. The APU hatches are open on all of the aircraft. The large Fowler flaps are extended, and the No. 1 and No. 2 engine cowl panels are removed on the aircraft in the foreground. Note how the national insignia is tangent with the aileron line. The forward top turrets were not initially installed on some B-29As due to a shortage. (Boeing X648)

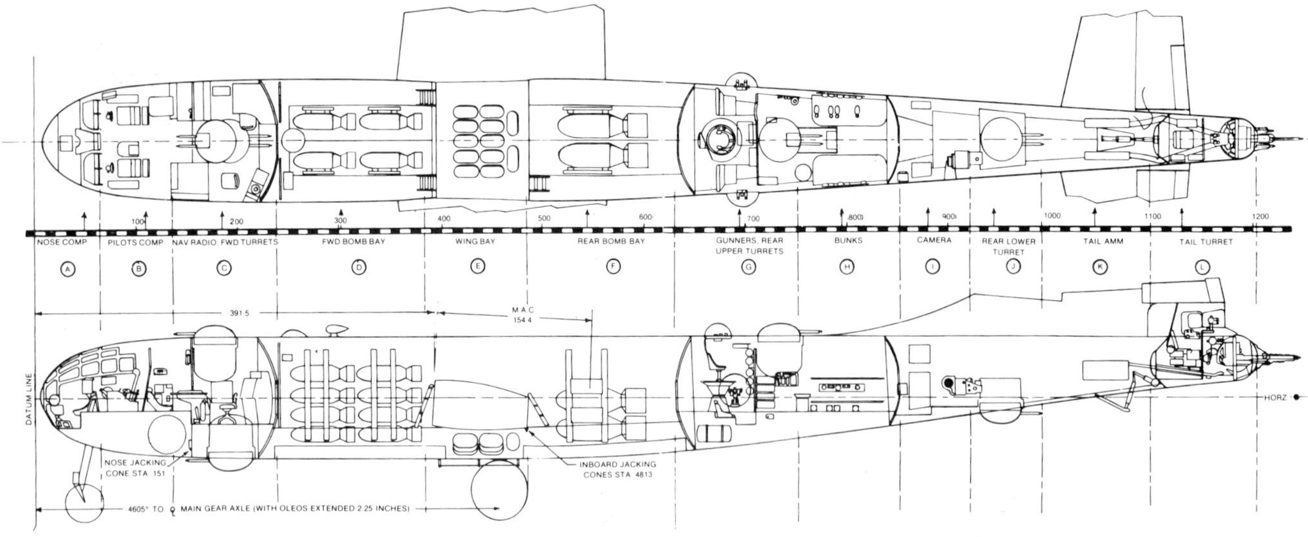

MAXIMUM INTERNAL BOMB LOAD

(4) 4000 LB BOMBS AND SHACKLES 16860 LBS
(8) 4000 LB BOMBS AND SHACKLES 16496 LBS
(4) 4000 LB BOMBS AND SHACKLES 16860 LBS
(8) 2000 LB BOMBS AND SHACKLES 16496 LBS
(12) 1600 LB BOMBS AND SHACKLES 19296 LBS
(12) 1000 LB BOMBS AND SHACKLES 11660 LBS
(40) 0500 LB BOMBS AND SHACKLES 20068 LBS
(56) 0300 LB BOMBS AND SHACKLES 16223 LBS
(80) 0100 LB BOMBS AND SHACKLES 10056 LBS

AMMUNITION

50 CALIBER WEIGHT PER 100 ROUNDS = 30 5 lbs
20 M M WEIGHT PER 100 ROUNDS = 55 0 LBS

B-29A INTERIOR ARRANGEMENT

Right side view of B-29A-75-BN, S/N 44-62312. Note the louvers on the supercharger access panel.
(Boeing 96568-B)

Black bellied B-29A-70-BNs undergoing completion at Boeing Field, across the hill from where they were built.
(Boeing 94054-B)

This B-29A-50-BN, S/N 44-61906, has the streamlined AN/APQ-13 belly radar antenna fairing installed.
(Boeing 91956-B)

B-29B

This view of B-29B-45-BA, S/N 44-843944, shows how clean the aircraft was without the turrets. The aircraft was assigned to the 331st BG, 315th BW. ***(Clyde Matteson)***

In a plant later to be occupied by the Lockheed-Georgia Company, Bell Aircraft built a total of 668 B-29s at their Marietta, Georgia plant. In order to meet the changing demands of the war in the Pacific, Bell produced 311 stripped down versions of the Superfortress designated B-29B. Based on the Boeing B-29, these aircraft carried the Boeing Model 345-3-0 designation. Numerous internal and external modifications were incorporated into the aircraft, most noticeable of which was the deletion of the remotely-sighted turrets. Between February and May 1945, Bell Aircraft delivered stripped aircraft to the Oklahoma City Air Depot for installation of a new electronic gear. Beginning in May 1945, Bell was capable of delivering completed aircraft.

Airplane modifications consisted of the following:

1. Power plant: Installation of revised engine baffles and louvered turbo supercharger well covers, and deletion of the pilots' throttle override controls.
2. Radio and electrical: Deletion of AN/ARR-1 homing adapter, SCR-718 radio altimeter, SCR-729 interrogator, portions of the SCR-274-N command radio, complete aft "Raven" station, frequency meter, search antennas and cables, and AN/APQ-13 radar. Redesigned static dischargers were incorporated to reduce drag.
3. Aircraft modifications: Deletion of all G-1 pressure signals and warning lights, one tail gunner's oxygen regulator, bunks and belts at auxiliary crew stations, bombardier's table, B-5 drift sight, engine covers, wiring diagram stowage boxes, oblique camera installation, and deicer boots (provisions retained).
4. Armament: Deletion of all four fuselage turrets, readily removeable turret structure, all fire control and associated turret equipment, 20 mm tail cannon, armor, except glass forward of pilots' position, and armor and glass aft of tail gunner, and flak protection, except Dural plate behind pilots' position. Installation of smooth covers for all turrets and sight openings, third .50 caliber machine gun in tail with maximum ammunition provisions, stowable .50 caliber machine guns in waist, and an AN/APG-15 gun laying radar coupled into the GE gun computer and IFF (Ella) equipment.
5. AN/APQ-7 "Eagle" Radar: Relocation of radar

Bell built B-29-45-BA at Renton in August 1946. The AN/APQ-7 Eagle radar antenna is mounted between the bomb bays. Cuffed Curtiss electric propellers are on engines No. 1 and 2 while Hamilton Standard hydromatic propellers are on engines No. 3 and 4. Note that this aircraft retains its turrets. (G. S. Williams)

Radar scope and controls for the AN/APQ-7 Eagle radar. (Clyde Matteson)

Three .50 caliber machine guns and the spherical antenna for the AN/APG-15 gun laying radar on a B-29B. (Clyde Matteson)

operator to forward crew compartment aft of navigator and opposite radio operator. No AN/APQ 7 repeater indicator was installed for the navigator. Deletion of the AN/ART-13 low frequency radio. A new A.C. power bus with two 2500 volt-ampere inverters was installed for added weight savings and system simplification. A "Nosmeagle" permitted coupling the Eagle radar with the Norden bombsight.

The Eagle radar was developed by the Radiation Laboratory of the Massachusetts Institute of Technology. Conceived in 1942, the length of time for development did not permit extensive use of the equipment in the European Theater. Several B-17s and approximately 20 B-24s received the installation and were used in tests for several months prior to the German surrender. In general, previous radar sets used in so-called "blind bombing" presented a 360° scan on the scope. At best the definition of the radar presentation was uncertain. With the Eagle radar, the beam was narrowed so that a 60° sector was presented on the scope, resulting in superior definition of the radar return. Externally the installation was readily recognizable by the 18-foot wide airfoil-shaped wing antenna suspended between the bomb bays.

Operational readiness requirements for the B-29B was so critical that there would be no delay in overseas movement of the aircraft and crews, and no waivers in training or equipment would be permitted with the exception of the AN/APG-15 gun laying radar, IFF, GE computer tie-in equipment, third tail gun, and waist guns. These aircraft were destined for the 315th Bomb Wing. Operational readiness for the 16th and 501st Bomb Groups was set for 1 April 1945, followed by the 502nd and 331st Bomb Groups on 1 May 1945. In order to maintain schedules, the radar operators were trained on B-24s equipped with the Eagle radar. After World War II the Eagle radar was removed from all operational B-29s.

B-29B FIVE VIEW DRAWING

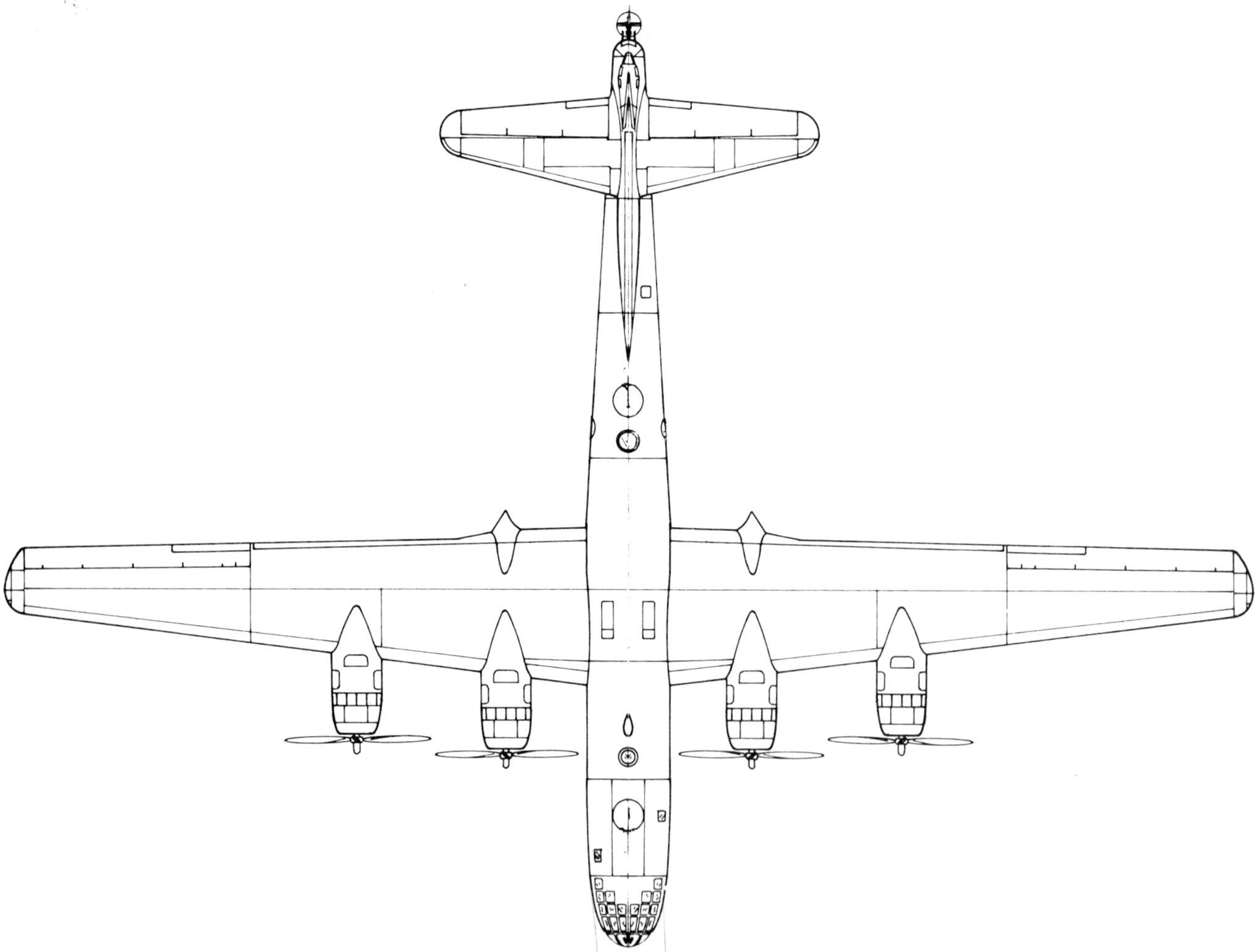

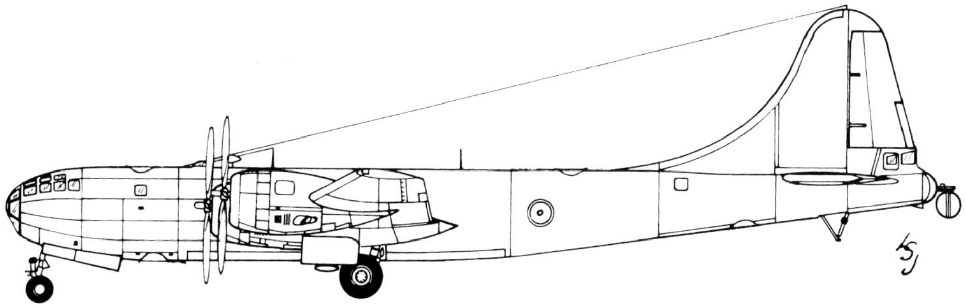

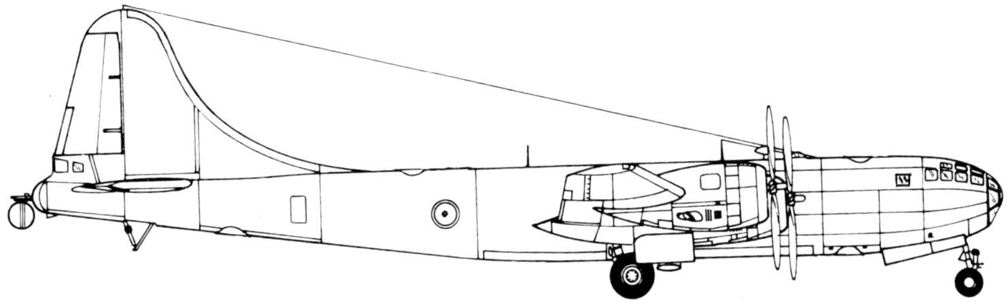

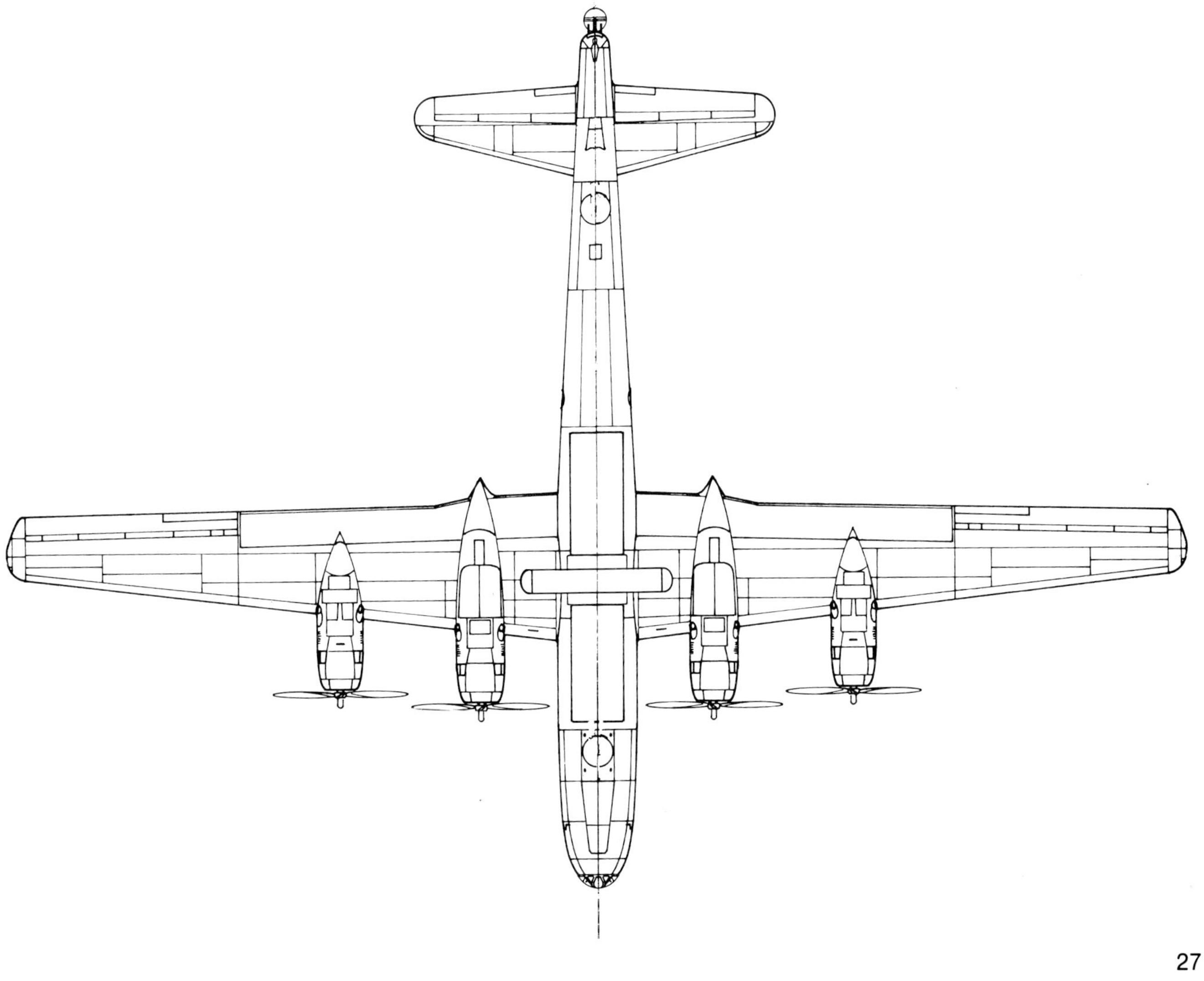

Bell built B-29-45-BA with Curtiss electric propellers turning and Hamilton Standards feathered in this pass over Renton Field. The AN/APQ-7 Eagle radar is visible on the belly as is AN/APQ-15 gun laying tail radar.
(G. S. Williams)

Late in the war the 8th Air Force was transitioning into B-29s. The newly formed 316th BW, comprised of the 333rd BG, 346th BG, and 382nd BG, and 383rd BG were to use B-29-BAs with the Eagle radar. These aircraft were fully armed and had the AN/APQ-15 gun laying radar. In these shots, one of the Bell built aircraft is shown taking off and making a pass with a Northrop P-61 Black Widow chase plane. The pictures were taken at Boeing Field.
(G.S. Williams)

B-29 STRUCTURAL DETAILS

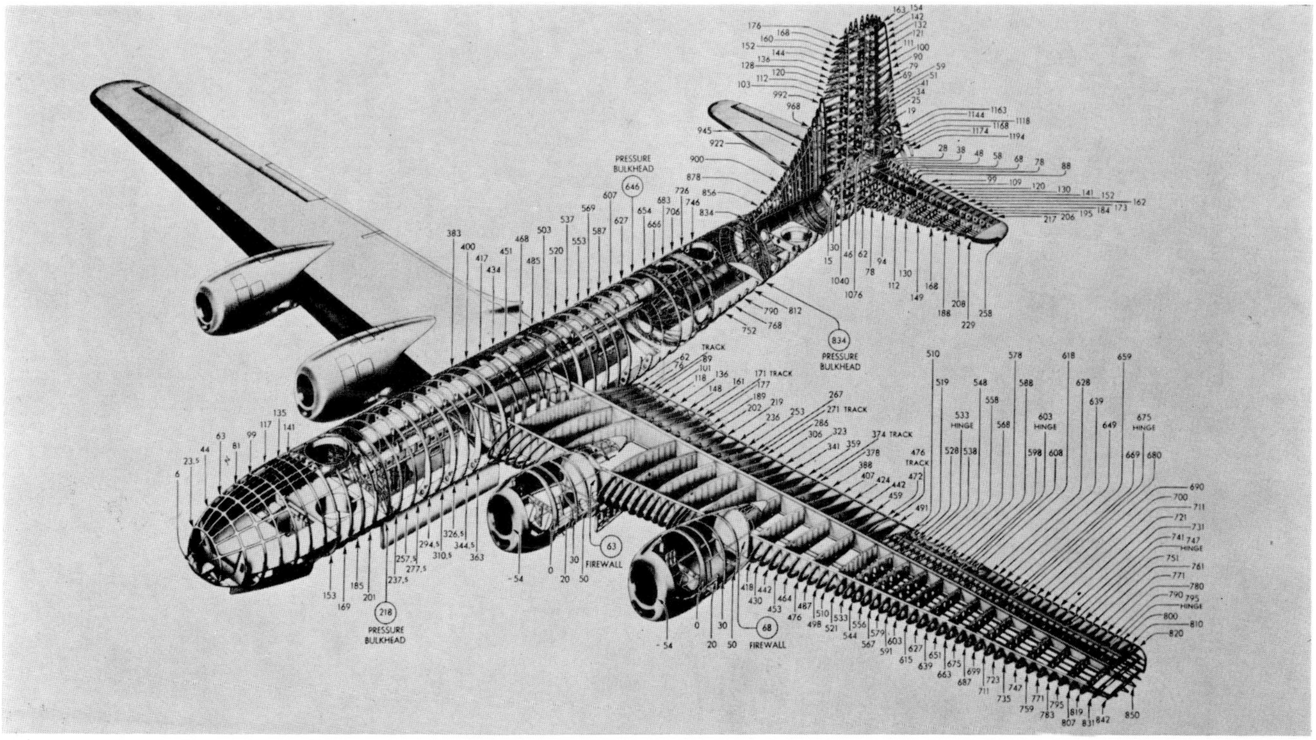

The major structural elements of the B-29 include the bulkheads, spars, and ribs. Station numbers are in inches. For the fuselage the station numbers run front to rear with Station 6 being the front of the nose piece and Station 1194 being the end of the tail turret. Circles enclose the major pressure bulkhead station numbers. Wing stations run outboard with 0 being at the airplane centerline, Station 62 is at the wing/fuselage join line, and Station 850 is at the wing tip. Nacelle stations run front to rear with Nac. Station -54 being the front of the cowl, Station 0 is the main bulkhead, Station 68 is the firewall. The horizontal and vertical stabilizers are similarly numbered. (Boeing HS 1420)

The inboard wing sections, bolted together at the center, are moved into position with a sling for installation on the first YB-29-BW, S/N 41-36954. Plumbing, control system components, and electrical wiring have already been installed on the wing subassemblies. (Boeing-Wichita BW-8517)

Major wing assembly on production B-29s at Wichita had the upper portion of the fuselage joined to the wing prior to mating with the fuselage. A portion of the communication tunnel is visible within the fuselage section. Completed nacelle and power packages were joined to the inboard wing sections at this stage of construction. (Boeing-Wichita BW23591)

A completed wing center section, replete with outboard power packages and main landing gear installed, is about to be mated with the unpressurized bomb bay section of the fuselage. (Boeing-Wichita BW282457)

Wings for the Renton-built B-29As had their inboard sections built-up with both the inboard and outboard power packages installed. Flaps were also incorporated at this time. The flange on the inboard edges of the wings in the foreground were used to bolt onto the stub wing center section. This method of wing buildup set the B-29As apart from all other B-29s. *(Boeing 56673-B)*

Renton-built B-29As in the final stages of assembly prior to factory rollout. *(Boeing P8512)*

In this striking night shot, B-29-45-BWs roll out of the factory. *(Boeing-Wichita BW23988)*

Completed Wichita built B-29s are shown on the flight line. The nacelle details are prevalent in this view. The first full aircraft shown is B-29-20-BW, S/N 42-6448. Next is the last of the -20 block, S/N 42-6454 followed by the first of the -25 block, S/N 42-24420. ***(Boeing-Wichita BW23089)***

A Clark tug is shown with a tow bar attached to the nose gear. The stenciling on the tow bar stowed on the tug states "No riders on tow bar". ***(Boeing 64386/BW17051)***

B-29 COLORS

The third XB-29-BO. Camouflaged control surfaces, commander's dome, and fin-mounted pitot tubes are visible. The yellowish tint on the wing inspar area appears to be zinc chromate primer. *(Boeing A54)*

One of the early camouflaged B-29-1-BWs, 42-6239. The de-icer boots have been removed. The 20 mm cannon is visible in the tail. *(Boeing A906)*

This view of a B-29A-30-BN, 42-94106, reveals the louvered supercharger panels. Note that the belly radome for the AN/APQ-13 radar has not been installed at this time. *(Boeing K-322)*

CUTAWAY DRAWINGS

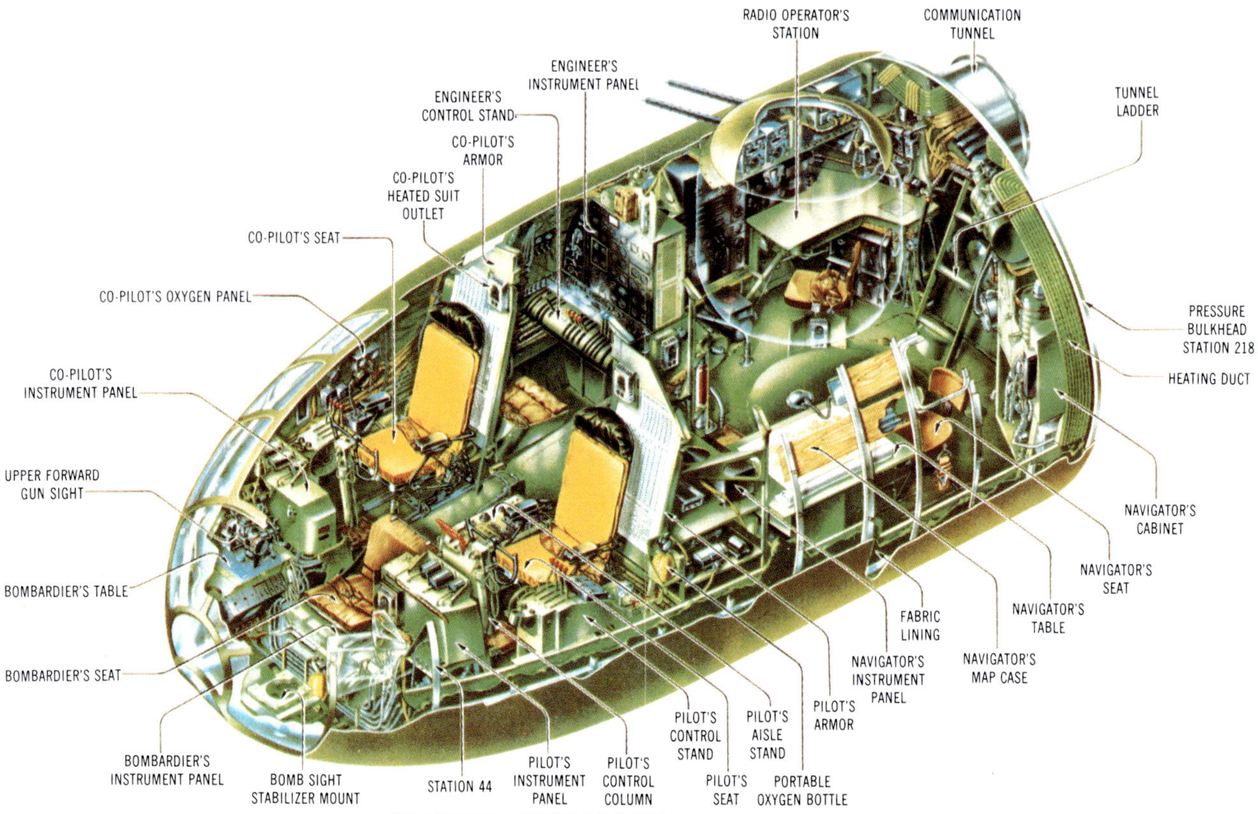

FORWARD PRESSURIZED COMPARTMENT

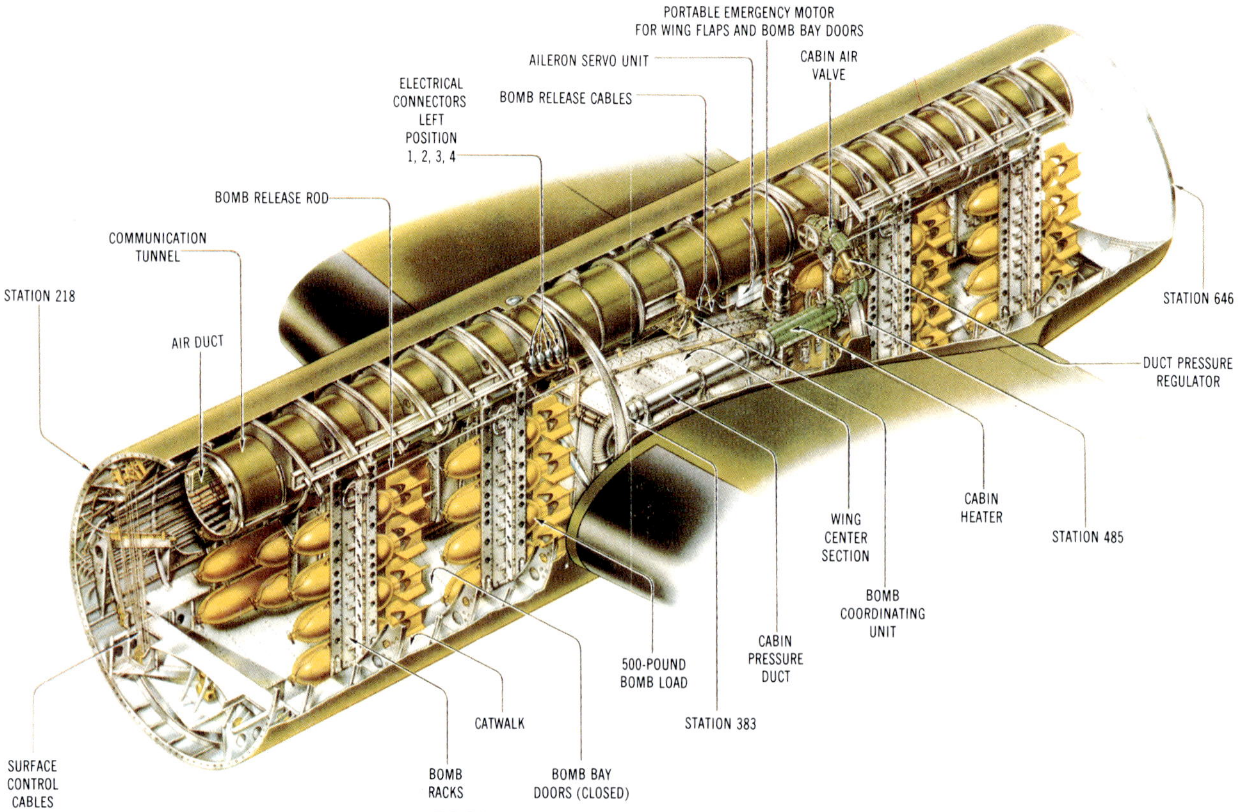

FORWARD AND AFT BOMB BAYS

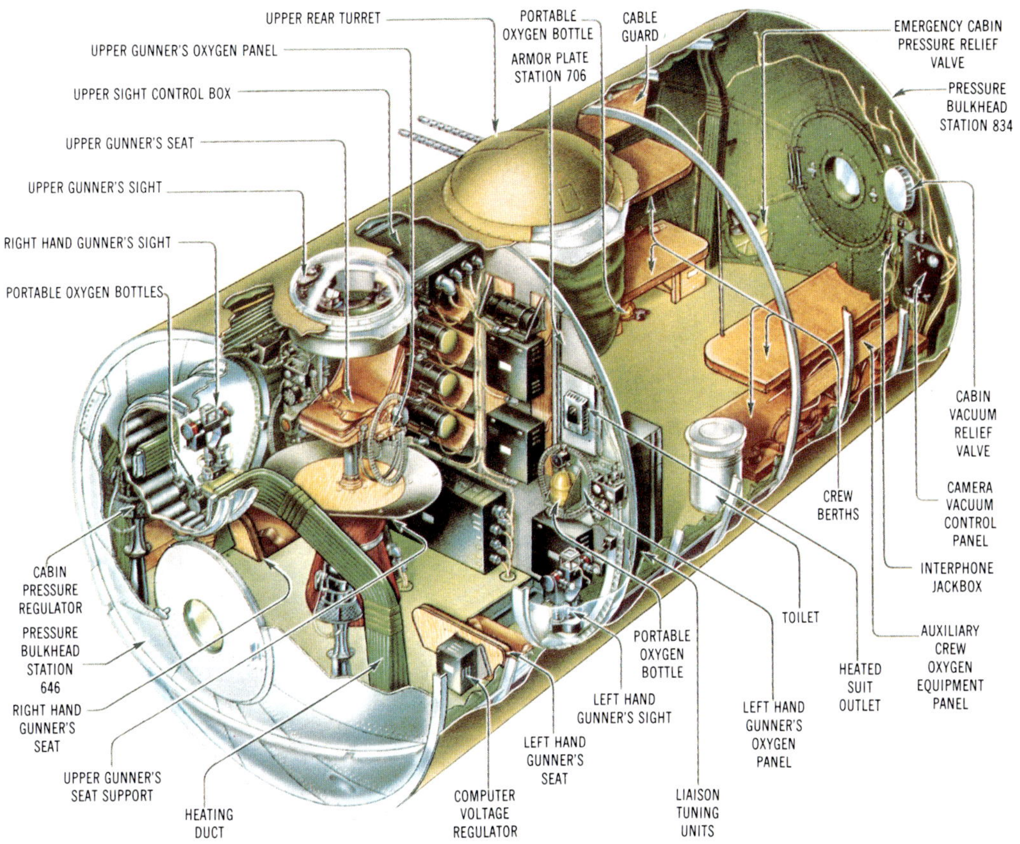

AFT PRESSURIZED COMPARTMENT

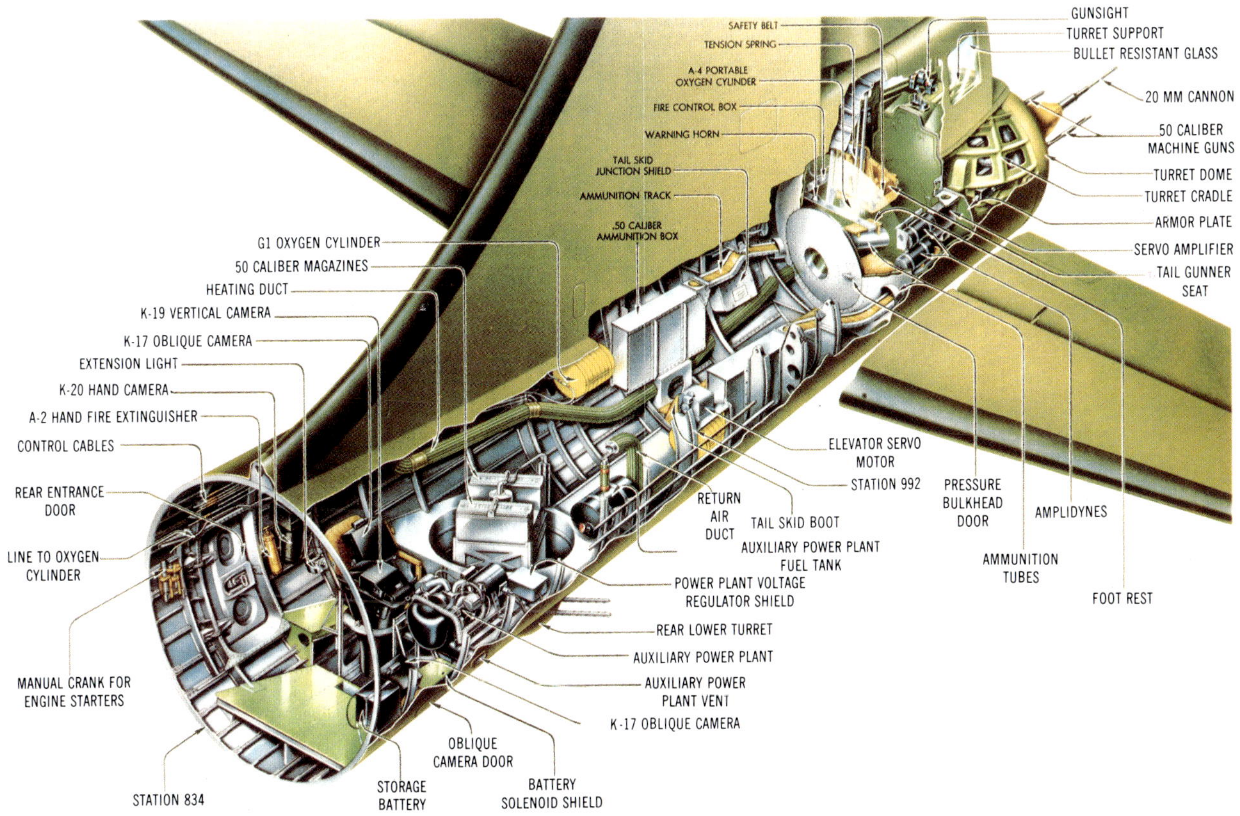

TAIL SECTION (UNPRESSURIZED) AND TAIL GUNNER'S COMPARTMENT

The color drawings on these two pages were taken from a B-29 Maintenance and Familiarization Manual (Boeing HS1006A-HS1006D)

INTERIOR COLORS

Looking forward between the pilot's and co-pilot's instrument panels at the bombardier's back. The bombardier is in the position he would assume when releasing the bombs on target. Note the plywood seat back for the bombardier. ***(Boeing 754)***

Pilot's station seen in flight. Chipped paint on the rudder pedal tube is the result of the tube being used as a footrest. Bulletproof glass is mounted above the instrument panel. ***(Boeing 744)***

Flight engineer's station. *(Boeing K751)*

Radar operator's station. *(Boeing K563)*

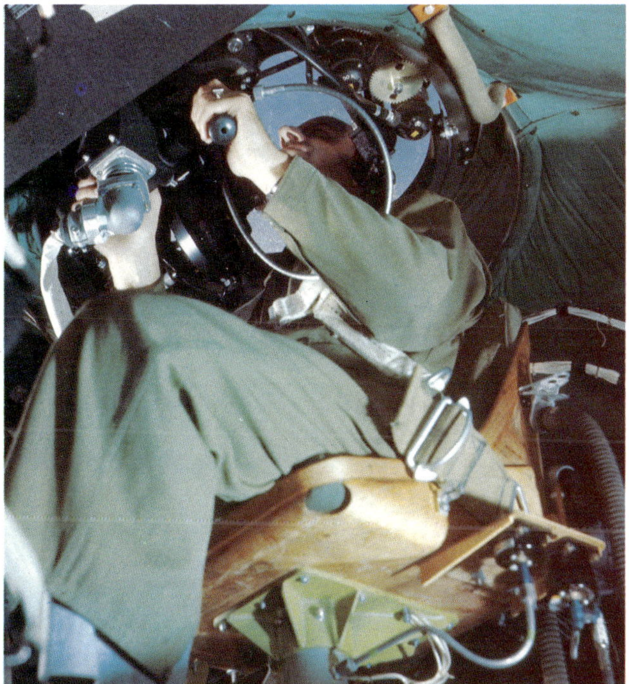

CFC gunner perched on his "barber's chair." *(Boeing K737)*

Right gunner's station. *(Boeing K742)*

EXTERIOR COLORS

This photo of a B-29A being towed shows skin panel shades to good effect. *(Williams)*

The brass shimmy damper cylinder is clearly visible in this view. An air temperature probe protrudes from the bombardier's nose, and cut-out lightening holes are visible inside the landing gear doors. *(Boeing K317)*

Number 3 engine details are revealed in this view. A data stencil is at the hub of each blade, and the yellow tips are six inches wide. *(Boeing K292)*

This photo of a B-29A during engine run-up reveals details of the upper and lower turrets, open bomb bay and landing gear doors, and skin panel details. (Williams)

Tail section details are visible in this photo to include the lower aft turret, tail bumper, rudder hinges, and tail gunner's door. (Williams)

In-flight view of B-29-45-BW, 42-24688. *(Boeing-Wichita TW-773-45C)*

B-29As on the assembly line at Renton, Washington. National insignia and tail numbers were applied to the various subsections. *(Boeing K535)*

COMMUNICATION SYSTEM

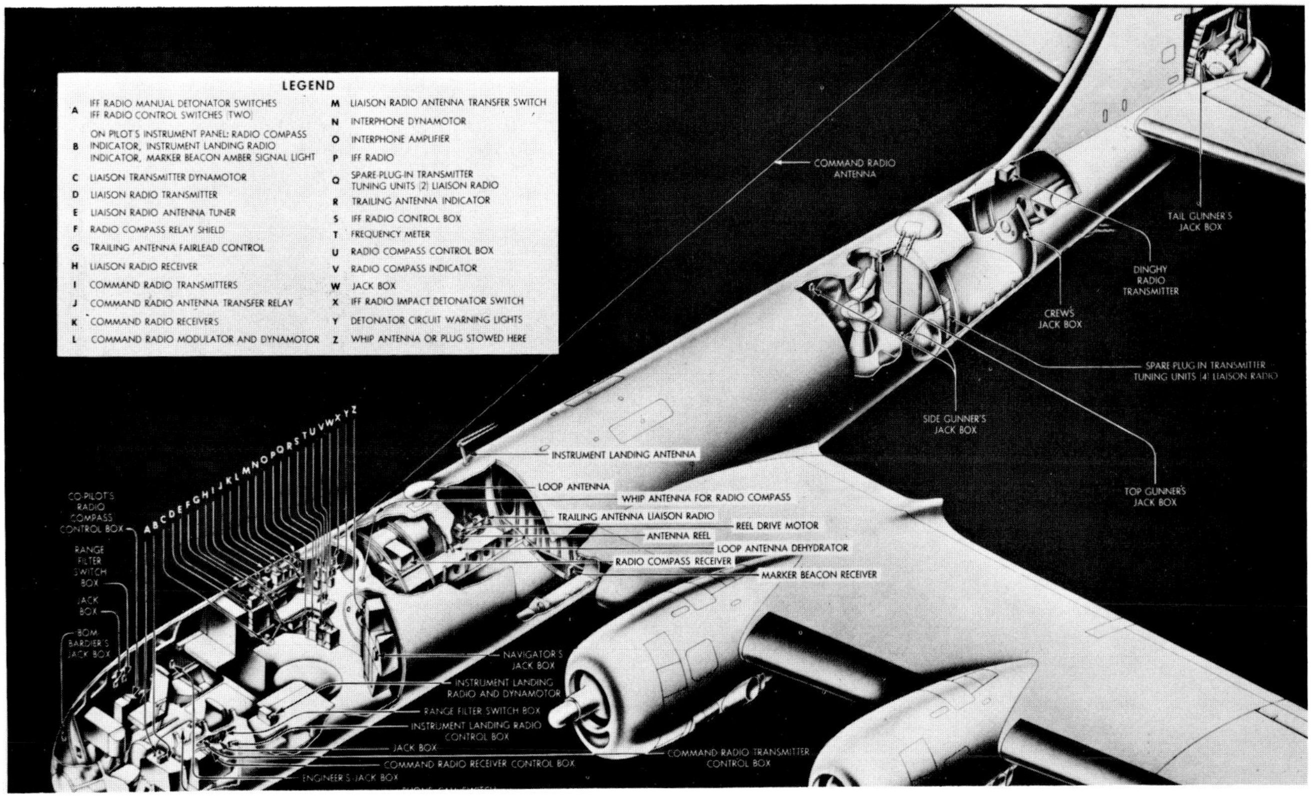

(Boeing HS1415)

FUEL SYSTEM

(Boeing HS1416)

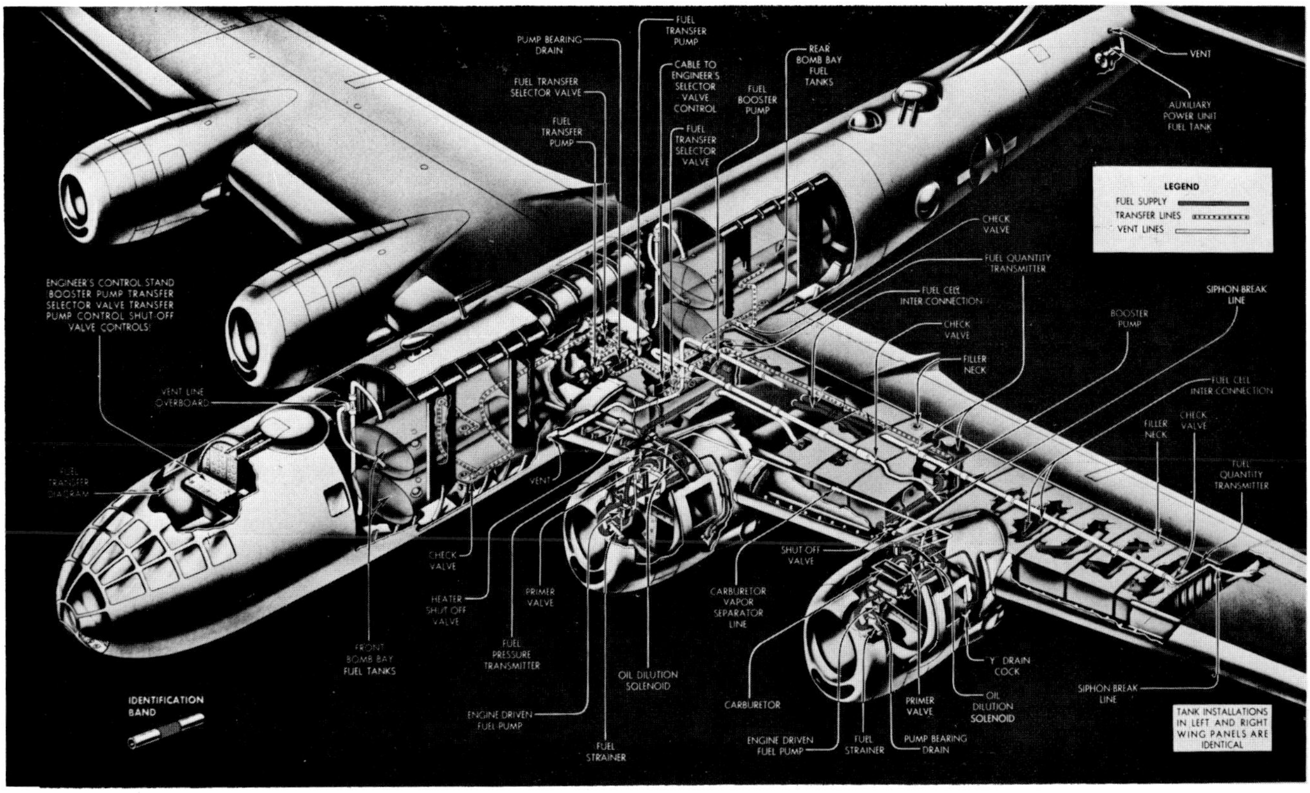

EXTERIOR LIGHTING

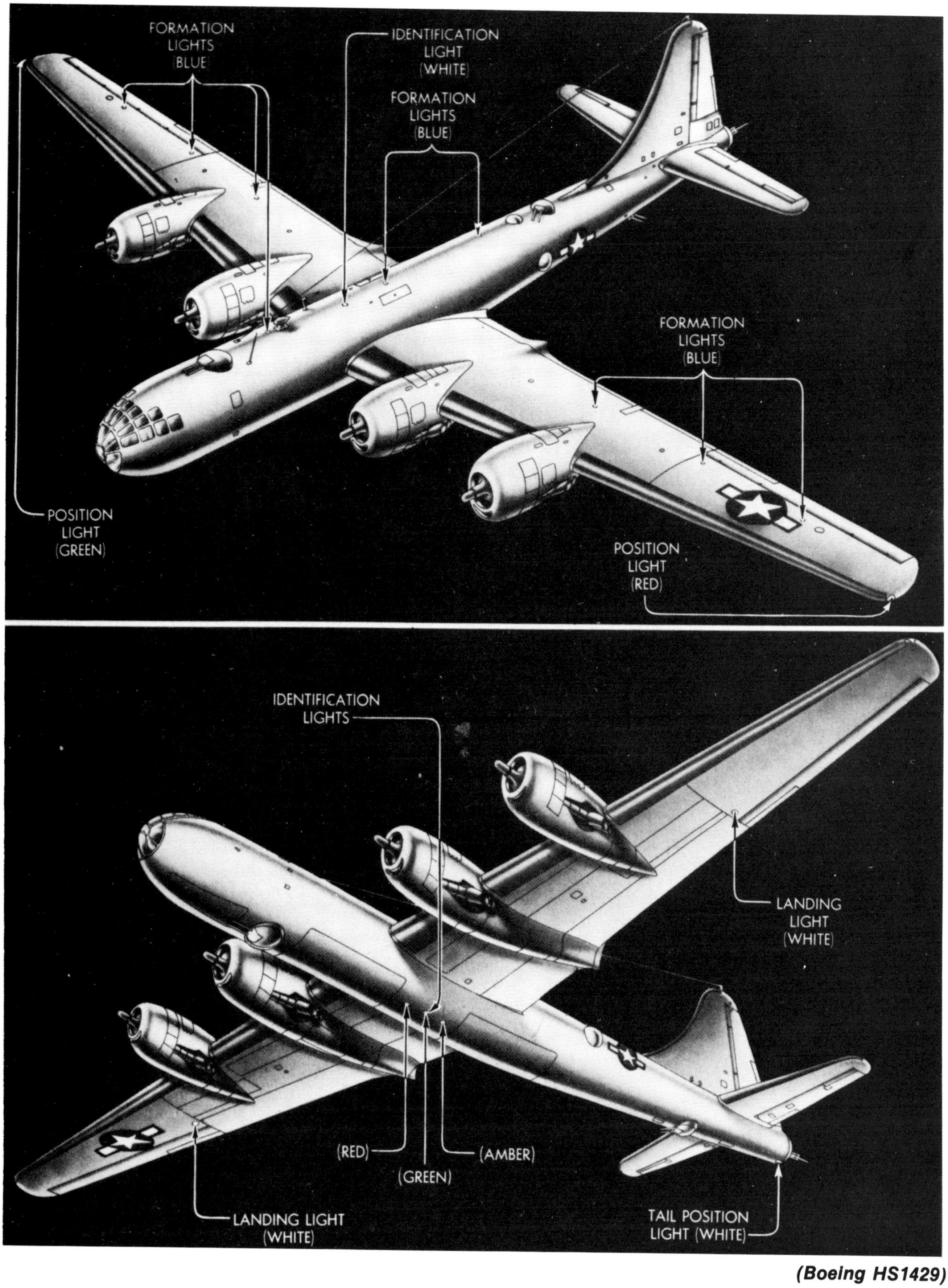

(Boeing HS1429)

ANTENNAS

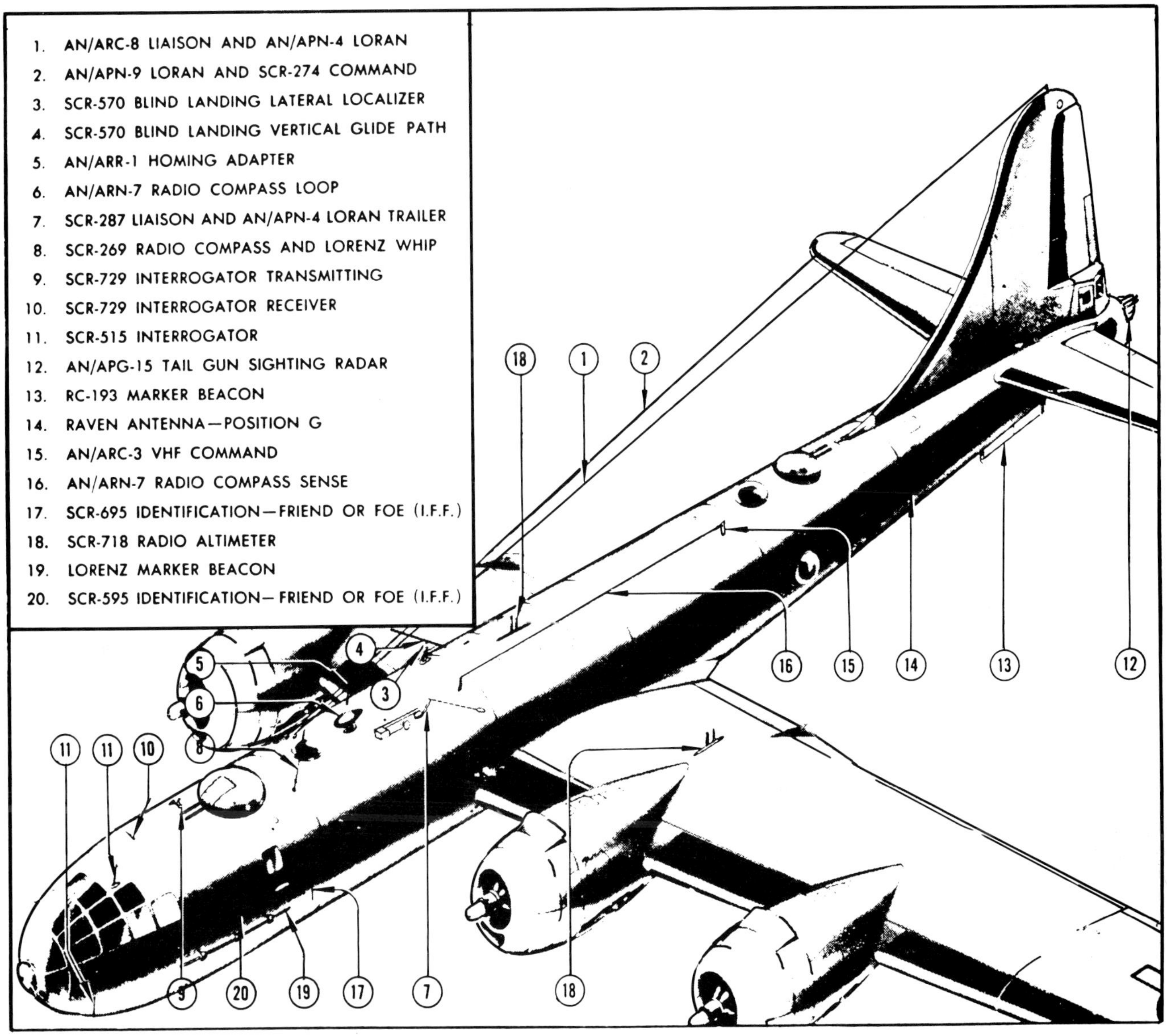

ALTERNATE INSTALLATIONS UNDER BOMB BAY

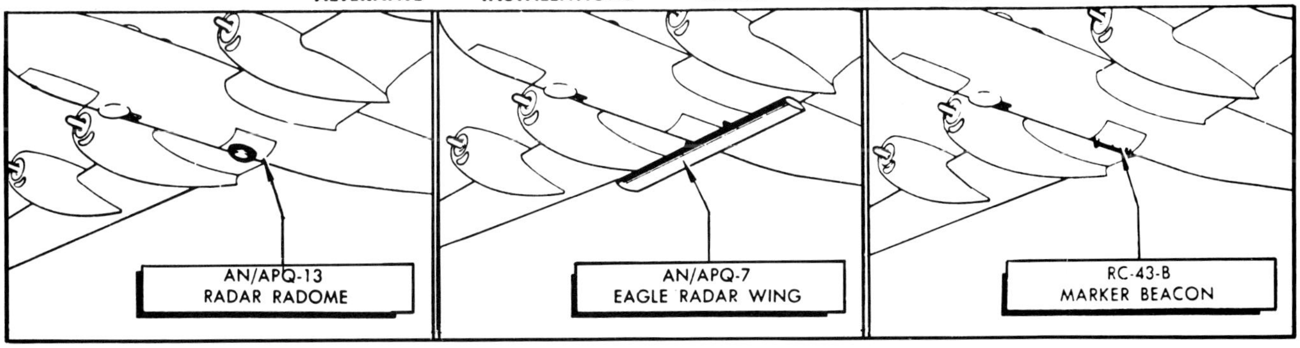

B-29 antennas after passing through USAAF modification centers. Antenna combinations varied by mission, unit assignment, and point in time. (Boeing HS1930)

LANDING GEAR DETAIL

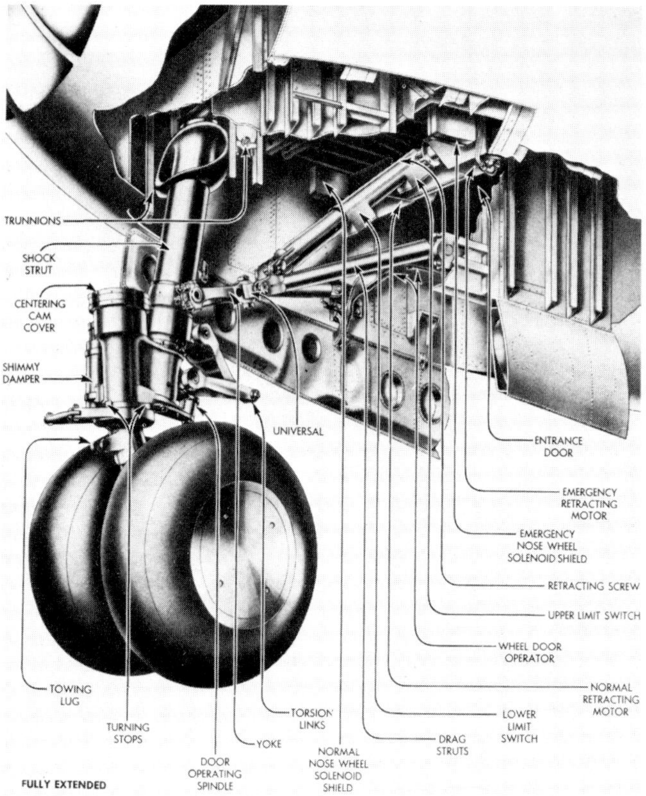

Nose Landing Gear Retraction Mechanism. ***(Boeing HS 1425)***

Rear view of nose landing gear. ***(Boeing 65139/BW-19458)***

Nose gear in the retracted position. The wheel door operator has been disconnected for this picture. The nose jack is visible on the right side of the photograph. ***(Boeing 64971/BW-19090)***

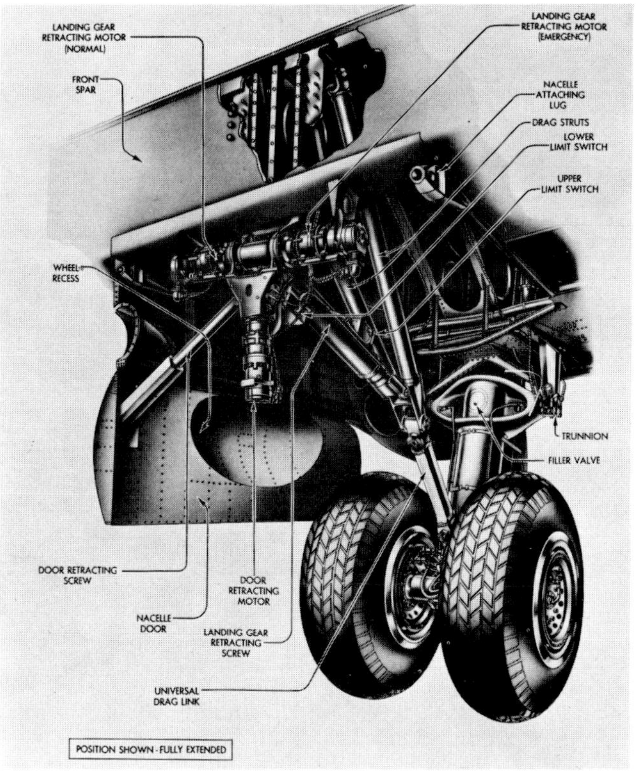

Main Gear Retracting Mechanism. (Boeing HS1418)

Main landing gear viewed from the rear. Torque links appear between the wheels. The strut door is located above the torque links. (Boeing 64966/BW19085)

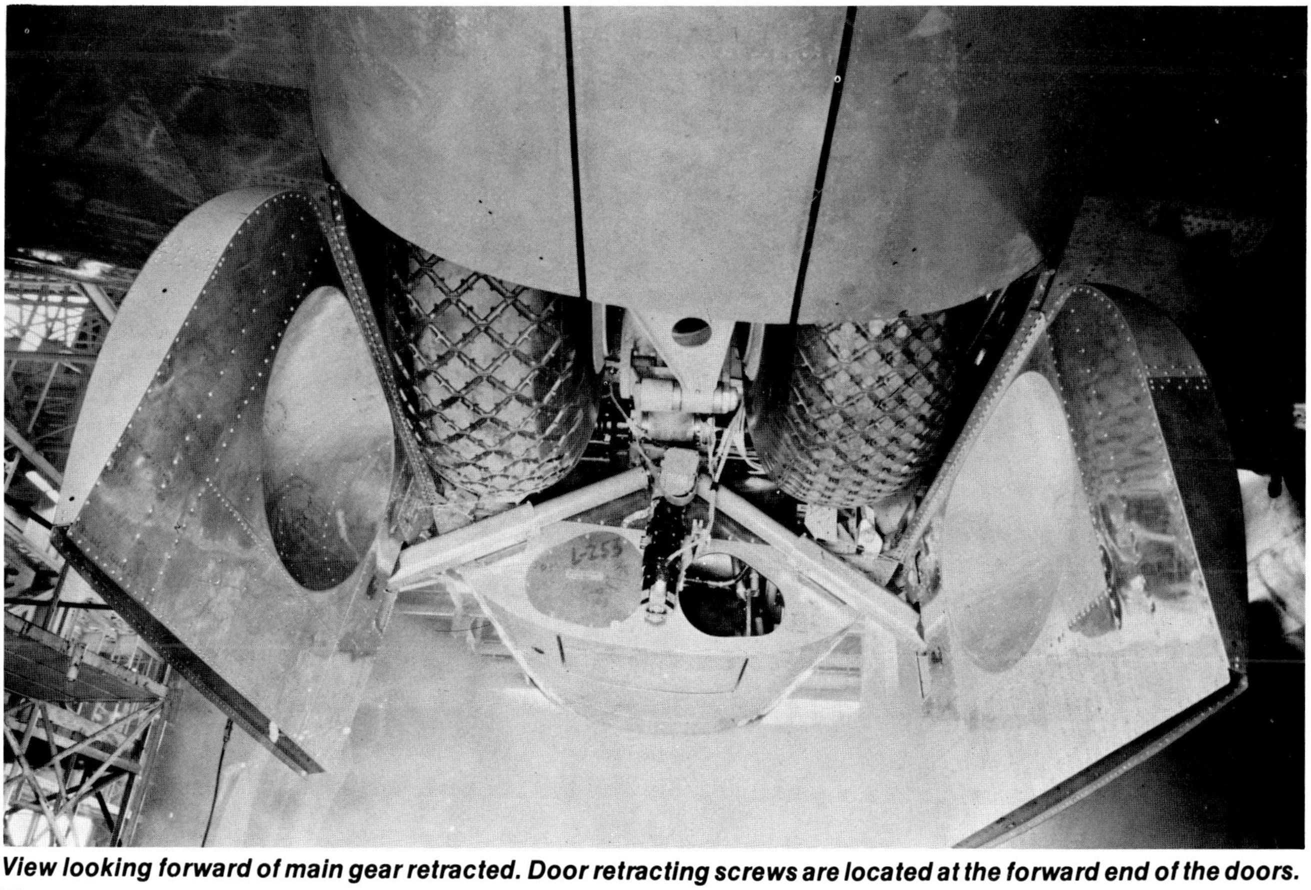

View looking forward of main gear retracted. Door retracting screws are located at the forward end of the doors. The strut cover is faired into position on the nacelle. (Boeing 64977/BW19096)

ENGINE INSTALLATION

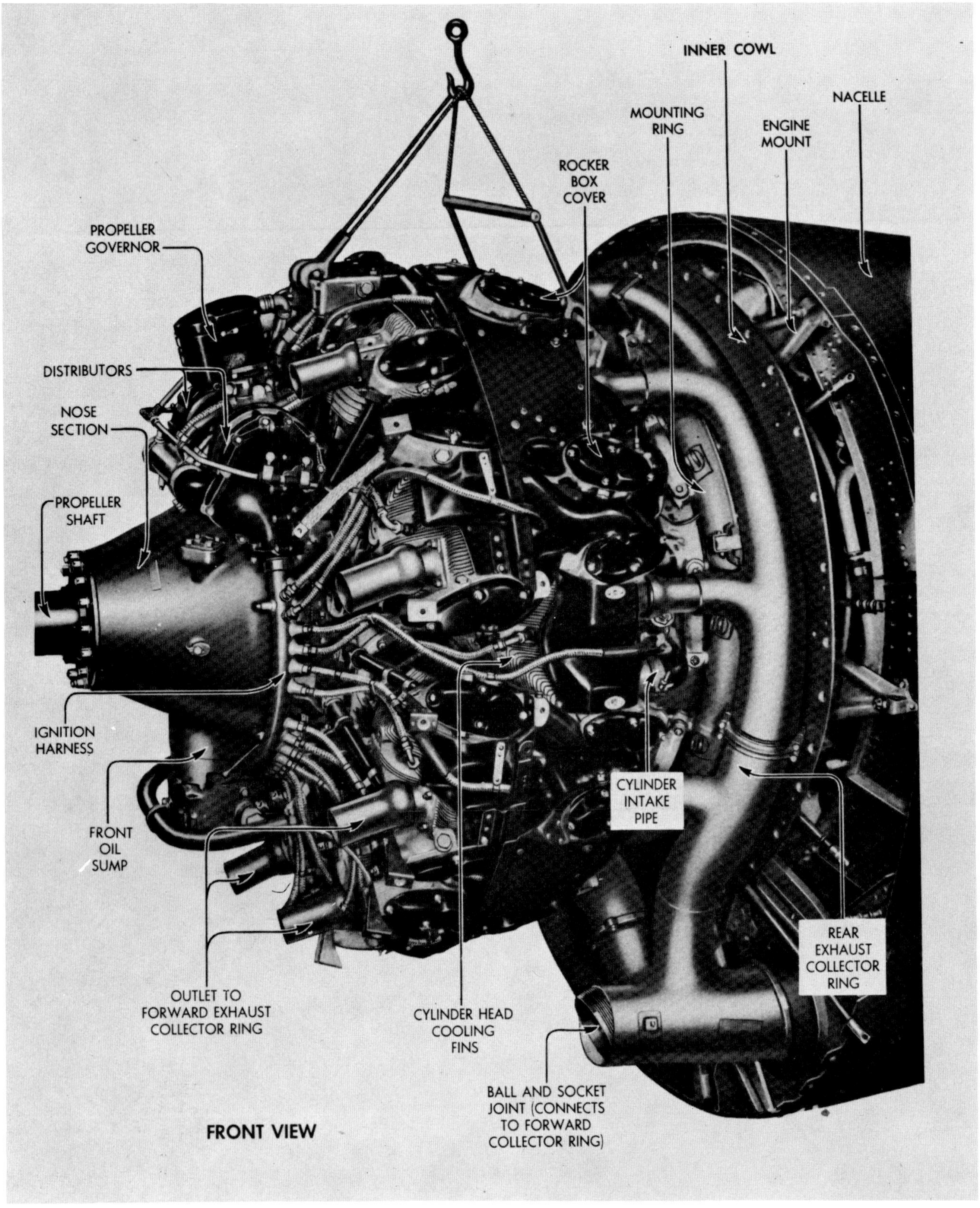

Engine Installation. The forward collector ring has been removed for clarity. ***(Boeing HS1417)***

Maintenance being performed on the Wright R-3350 engine in the field. The initial design was such that the propeller and cowling had to be removed in order to perform the simplest tasks, including spark plug changes. The turbo supercharger is located aft of the engine, behind the firewall. (Marvin Hooker)

The No. 3 engine with its huge 16'7" diameter Hamilton Standard hydromatic propeller. A Hamilton Standard decal is located at the center of each blade. Stenciling at the hub end of each blade gives the propeller specifications. The steel blades were painted flat black and had a 6-inch yellow tip. (Boeing X884)

By contrast, the Curtiss electric propellers had a different prop hub and dome. The blades were highly contoured by comparison, and had cuffs added to improve the engine cooling. (John Gahagan)

INTERIOR DETAILS

Pilot, co-pilot, and bombardier stations on XB-29-BO, S/N 41-003. The vacant space in the aisle stand is for the autopilot controls. Note that there are no instruments mounted above the pilot's instrument boards as found on production aircraft. A standard Boeing "horn button" is installed on each control wheel. (Boeing 35887-B)

The prized "horn button" is visible on the pilot's control wheel. A cover is on the then secret Norden bombsight. Propeller controls, autopilot controls, radio switches, and some bomb controls are located on the aisle stand. (Boeing X317)

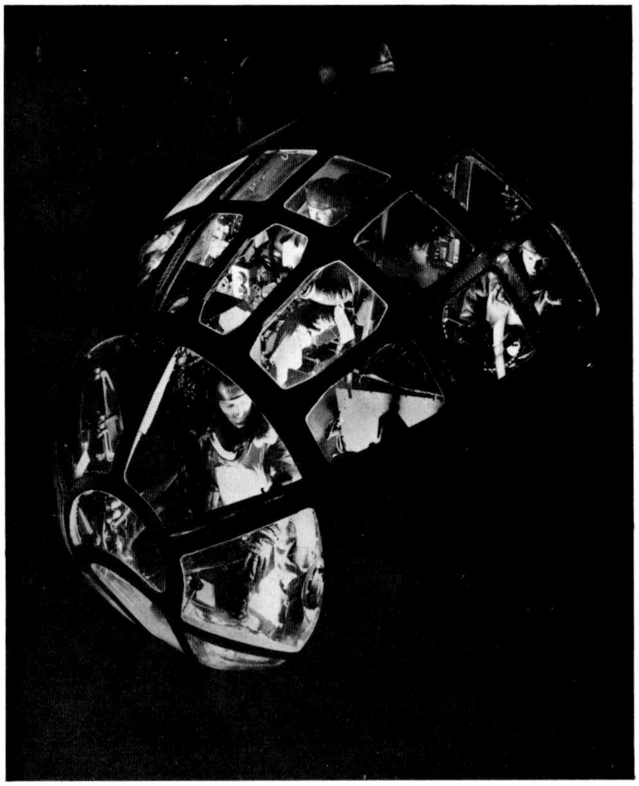

Cockpit details become more apparent in this "night" mock-up shot. (Boeing X563)

Pilot's station showing aisle stand, controls, instruments, pilot's seat, and stowed bombardier's seat. Outside air temperature gauge is located on bombardier's greenhouse. Note nose glass deicing tube. 300 mph maximum airspeed placard is located above the flight instruments -- airspeed, needle/ball, and rate of climb. (Boeing X314)

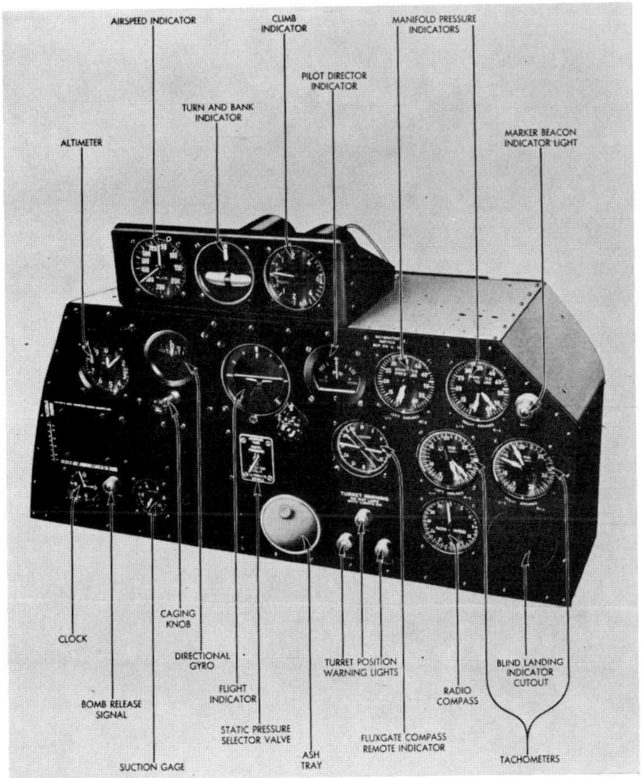

Pilot's main instrument board. The primary flight instruments were mounted on top of the basic panel. (Boeing HS1422)

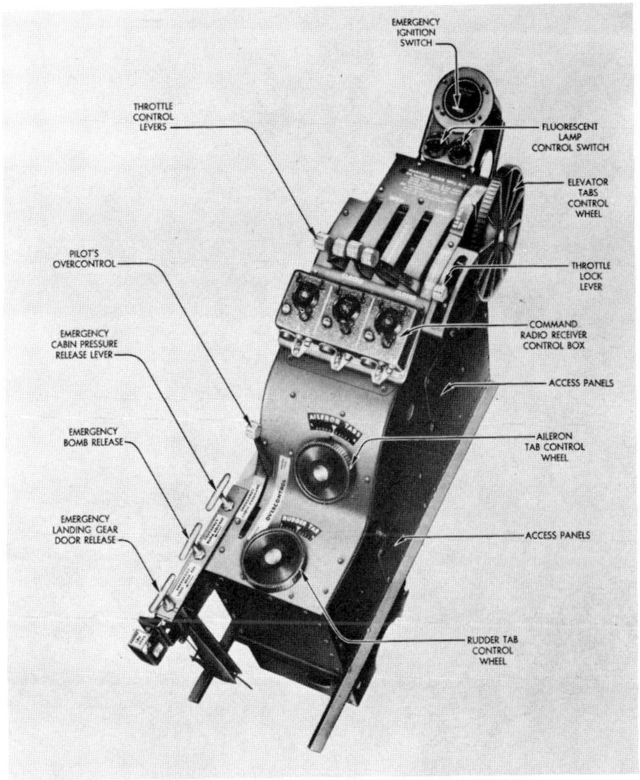

The pilot's control stand was located outboard of the seat. A mirror image control stand was located on the co-pilot's side of the aircraft. (Boeing HS1423)

Pilot's side of the front "office". Flip-up arm rests allowed easier ingress and egress for the pilot. The "horn button" has not been installed on this aircraft -- they were the last item put on the aircraft at delivery and it is not known how many of them ever remained on operational aircraft. The sliding window is located just behind the pilot's head. Pilot's hand is on the parking brake handles. A placard on the instrument board would indicate that this aircraft is a Renton built B-29A. *(Boeing X392)*

Copilot's station. Throttles are visible on side console. Famed "horn button" has been installed on the control wheel. Radio call placard below DG compass identifies this airplane as B-29A-5-BN 42-93846. Elevator trim wheel is prominently in view. *(Boeing X313)*

The flight engineer's station was located directly behind the co-pilot. The seat faced aft. B-29 flight engineers during WW II were officers. Their skill at this station was soon appreciated by the pilots who learned to rely on them for getting the cantankerous R-3350 engines started and for nursing the crippled aircraft home.
(Boeing 55701-B)

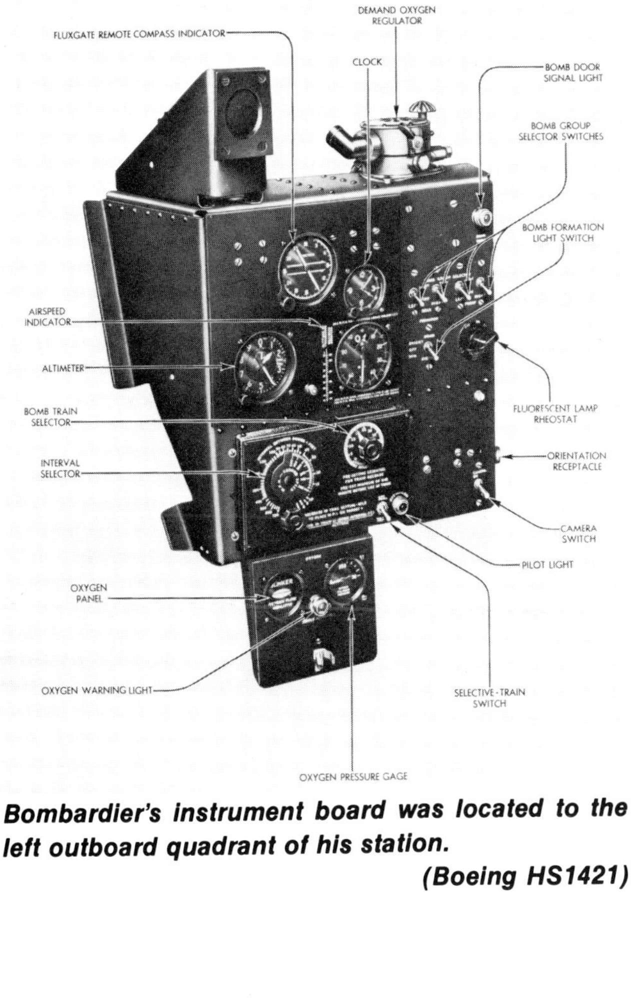

Bombardier's instrument board was located to the left outboard quadrant of his station.
(Boeing HS1421)

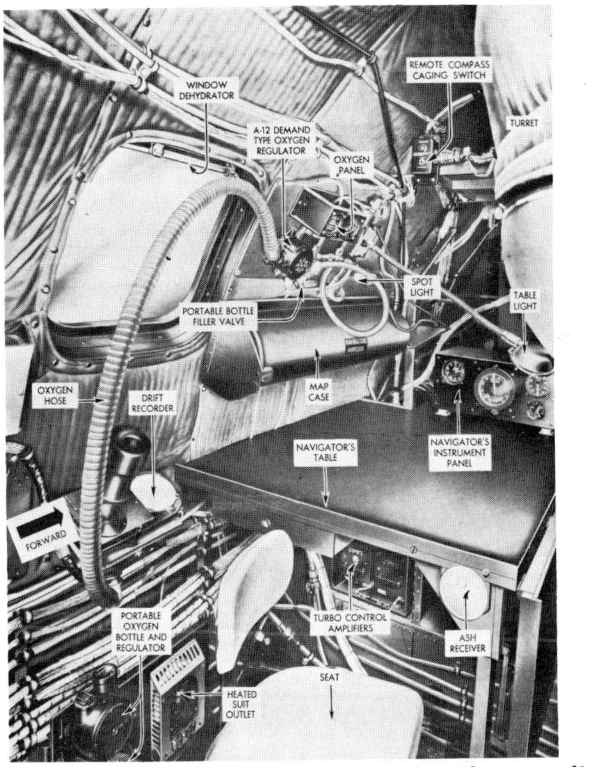

The navigator's station was located directly opposite the flight engineer, behind the pilot. The drop leaf on the inboard end of the table allowed additional room for laying out the charts. ***(Boeing HS1426)***

On most B-29s the radar observer's station was located in the aft pressurized compartment on the left side just ahead of the aft pressure bulkhead. This position was also blind. The duty of this officer was to track enemy radio and radar and use his ECM gear to jam the radar. Varying mast antennas were installed on the aft fuselage for his equipment. This position was moved forward to a location behind the navigator on the B-29Bs. *(Boeing-Wichita BW24364)*

The radio operator's station was located aft of the flight engineer's station. There were no windows for this station. *(Boeing 55703-B)*

Unusual view looking aft from the cockpit. Hatch to nose wheel well makes up floor panel in foreground. A portion of the flight engineer's panel is visible on the left. Large padded structure is the forward top turret. Pressure bulkhead leads to the forward bombbay. Radio operator's station is located behind the flight engineer. Domed floor panel houses the forward lower turret. *(Boeing X319)*

CFC gunner's position. *(Boeing X321)*

View into tail gunner's station. Lower turret ammunition boxes are in the center of this picture. Black APU fuel tank is on the right. Oxygen bottles and tail gun ammunition cans are visible on either side of the pressure bulkhead hatch. *(Boeing X321)*

Crew rest area in the aft pressurized section. *(Boeing X711)*

OFFENSIVE ARMAMENT

Cargo pallets are installed in the bomb bays of this B-29A-5-BN. *(G. S. Williams)*

B-29A-5-BN with bomb bay doors open. *(G. S. Williams)*

View looking forward on this B-29A-5-BN with electric bomb bay door actuators. Cargo pallets are installed in the bomb bay. Notches in flaps are to afford flap track clearance when the flaps are retracted.(Boeing X339)

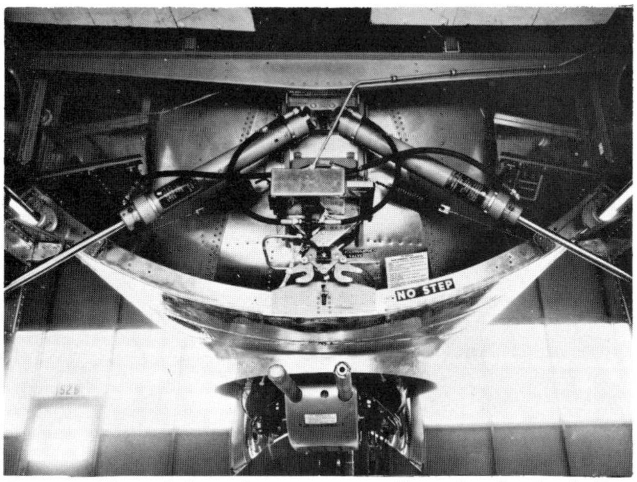

Forward bomb bay door pneumatic actuator installation. The door up lock latches are visible in the center of the picture. Front bottom turret dome has not been installed. (Boeing 68227/BW31454)

Aft bomb bay door pneumatic actuator installation. The early AN/APQ-13 belly radar antenna fairing appears below the door up lock latches. (Boeing 68222/BW31449)

Left side 1000-pound bomb rack in the forward bomb bay. (Boeing 54796-B)

Looking aft at 1000-pound bomb racks in front bomb bay. Control cable, plumbing, and wire bundle runs appear along the sides of the fuselage. The communication tube is located in the top center of the picture. Black ends of the wing center section fuel tanks are readily apparent in this view. Three bomb bay lights are visible in the picture; the fluorescent lamps are shop work lamps. (Boeing 54795-B)

Looking aft at racks in aft bomb bay. The door in the pressure bulkhead leads to the aft crew compartment. (Boeing 54798-B)

DEFENSIVE ARMAMENT

Upper gun turret and fairing. This twin gun installation was common to all four positions prior to the change over to the four-gun front top turret. Dome removal instructions are on the placard.
(Boeing 53253-B)

Late model B-29As had this tear-drop shaped top front turret which was also installed on later model B-50s. The astrodome is located behind the turret. Note the wire antenna mount ahead of the turret.
(Boeing 96562-B)

Later B-29s were equipped with the four-gun front top turret. The contour follower may be seen between the center guns. A temperature probe is located aft of the flight engineer's emergency exit hatch.
(Boeing-Wichita BW29382)

Front lower turret is turned and guns are depressed to clear bomb bay doors and nose gear doors. The square cross-section on the bomb bay door actuators indicates that these were of the earlier electric jackscrew type. The oxygen bottles may be seen above the belly skin between the bomb bays. Later, the AN/APQ-13 radar antenna and fairing would be installed on this skin panel. *(Boeing X387)*

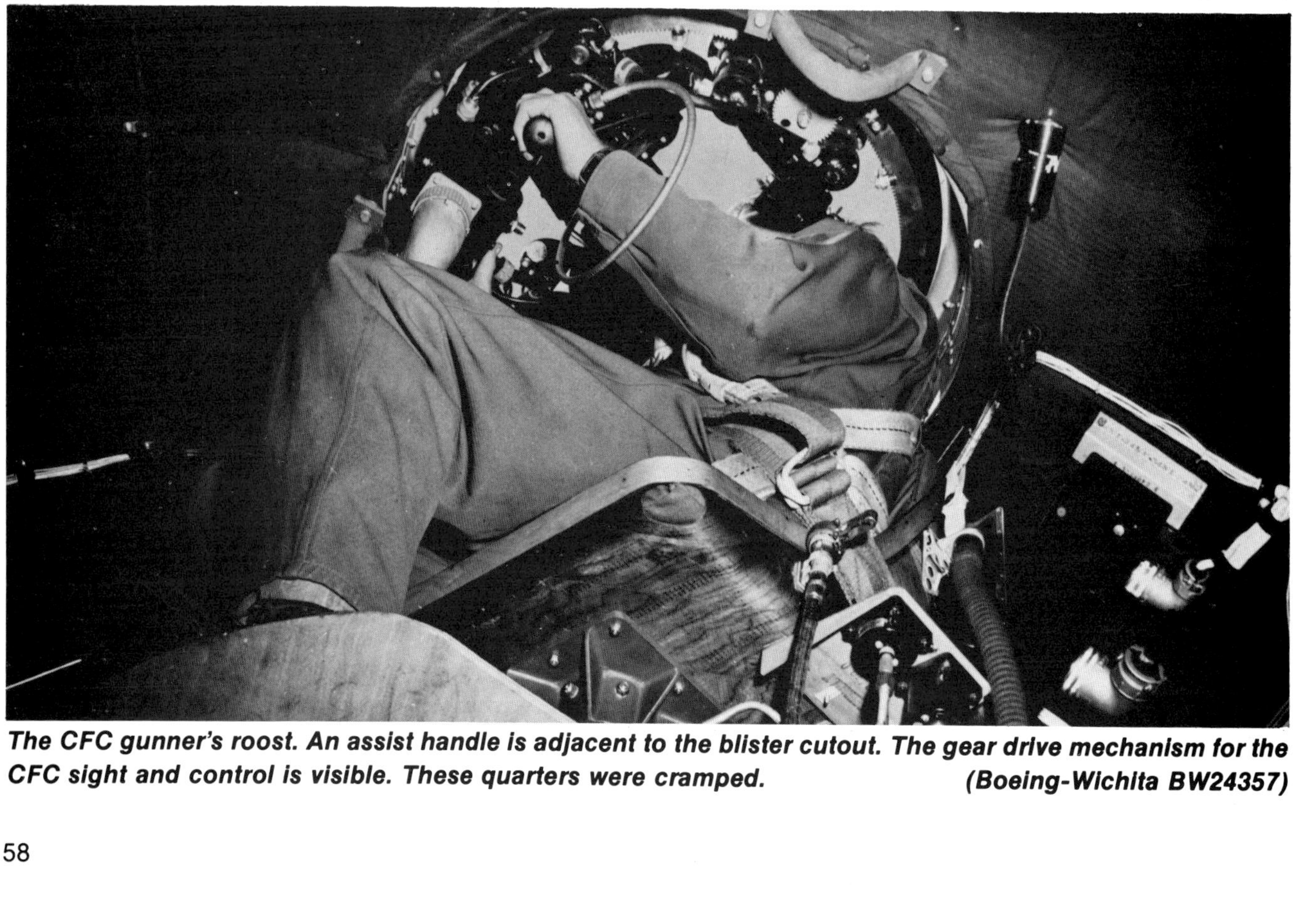

The CFC gunner's roost. An assist handle is adjacent to the blister cutout. The gear drive mechanism for the CFC sight and control is visible. These quarters were cramped. *(Boeing-Wichita BW24357)*

Side gunner demonstrates use of his pedestal-mounted gun sight. *(Boeing-Wichita BW24476)*

Exterior view of left hand pedestal-mounted side gunner's sight. Note the placard CUT THRU GLASS FOR EMERGENCY RESCUE. After the loss of blisters in flight, the retention structure was beefed up.
(Boeing X1261)

Right side of aft fuselage reveals the CFC sighting blister, right waist blister, upper and lower aft turrets, and the aft entry door. ***(Boeing X374)***

Aft top turret and right sighting blister. ***(Boeing K727)***

CFC gunner in sighting position. Aft top turret reveals the camera port between the guns. A reinforcing fairing has been added around the turret. ***(Boeing X381)***

Early tail gun installation with protective boots over the twin .50 caliber machine guns and the 20 mm cannon. This installation is on the first B-29A-5-BN. ***(Boeing X340)***

Uncovered tail guns showing canvas turret boot and spent shell case chute beneath turret. The bomb release formation light is visible above the gunner's window. ***(Boeing X385)***

EXPERIMENTAL ARMAMENT

For special operations in the Pacific an experimental bomb rack was developed and tested on the B-29-75-BW, S/N 44-70060. Four 4,000-pound bombs were carried on external racks which could also accommodate other combinations of airborne TNT, including 22,000-pound bombs. With these "Grand Slam" bombs carried externally, the B-29 was capable of carrying its normal internal bomb load or bomb bay fuel tanks. This installation never saw combat. (Boeing 95560)

A pair of 22,000-pound "Grand Slam" bombs could be carried on the external racks developed by Boeing-Wichita. This project was developed for use against special targets on the Japanese mainland; however, it was never used in combat. (Boeing 95561)

B-20-25-BW, S/N 42-24441, was extensively modified for the Project S68 manned turret evaluation in October 1944. The project was soon scrapped.

Front view of remotely controlled Emmerson Model 136 jowl barbettes with single .50 caliber machine guns. (Boeing 83583-B)

Left side view of the nose shows the Emmerson barbettes, Martin upper forward turret, and Sperry A-2 ball turret. (Boeing 83590-B)

Rear armament was changed to a Martin upper aft turret, Sperry A-13 ball turret, and flexible .50 caliber gun in the waist station. *(Boeing 83589-B)*

Close-up of the aft lower Sperry A-13 (modified) ball turret in the retracted position. A standard turret was modified to have a shorter hanger than was used on the B-24 and B-32. *(Boeing 83588-B)*

Interior view of the right hand waist gun installation. Plywood box contained the ammunition. Spent shell casings and links were collected in the canvas basket beneath the gun. *(Boeing A9890)*

Martin upper aft turret installation without the plexiglas dome. This photo was taken on the east apron of Boeing Field on 10 August 1944. *(Boeing A9452)*

Interior view of the tail turret installation showing ammunition chutes. The tail gunners' compartment pressure hatch is shown in the open position. *(Boeing A20202)*

"RAVEN" ANTENNAS

Left and right side views of "Raven" radio countermeasures antennas bristling from the aft fuselage. Antenna arrays were changed to suit specific mission requirements. ***(USAF via D. Q. Roberts)***

B-29 PRODUCTION BLOCKS AND SERIALS

This newly completed B-29A-70-BN has the tear-drop shapped upper front turret. ***(Boeing 96570-B)***

BLOCK	SERIAL
XB-29-BO	41-002/41-003
XB-29-BO	41-18335
YB-29-BW	41-36954/41-36967
B-29-1-BW	42-6205/42-6221
B-29-1-BA	42-6222
B-29-1-BW	42-6223
B-29-1-BA	42-6224
B-29-1-BW	42-6225/42-6228
B-29-1-MO	42-6229/42-6232
B-29-1-BA	42-6233
B-29-1-BW	42-6234
B-29-1-BA	42-6235
B-29-1-BW	42-6236
B-29-1-MO	42-6237
B-29-1-BW	42-6238/42-6242
B-29-1-BA	42-6243
B-29-1-BW	42-6244/42-6254
B-29-5-BW	42-6255/42-6304
B-29-10-BW	42-6305/42-6354
B-29-15-BW	42-6355/42-6404
B-29-20-BW	42-6405/42-6454
B-29-25-BW	42-24420/42-24469
B-29-30-BW	42-24470/42-24519
B-29-35-BW	42-24520/42-24569
B-29-40-BW	42-24570/42-24669
B-29-45-BW	42-24670/42-24769
B-29-50-BW	42-24770/42-24869
B-29-55-BW	42-24870/42-24919
B-29-1-BA	42-63352/42-63365
B-29-5-BA	42-63366/42-63381
B-29-10-BA	42-63382/42-63401
B-29-15-BA	42-63402/42-63451
B-29-20-BA	42-63452/42-63501
B-29-25-BA	42-63502/42-63551
B-29-30-BA	42-63552/42-63580
B-29B-30-BA	42-63581/42-63621
B-29B-35-BA	42-63622/42-63691
B-29B-40-BA	42-63692/42-63736
B-29-40-BA	42-63737
B-29B-40-BA	42-63738/42-63743
B-29-40-BA	42-63744
B-29B-40-BA	42-63745/42-63749
B-29-40-BA	42-63750
B-29B-40-BA	42-63751

BLOCK	SERIAL
B-29-1-MO	42-65202/42-65204
B-29-5-MO	42-65205/42-65211
B-29-10-MO	42-65212/42-65219
B-29-15-MO	42-65220/42-65235
B-29-20-MO	42-65236/42-65263
B-29-25-MO	42-65264/42-65313
B-29-30-MO	42-65315/42-65401
B-29A-1-BN	42-93824/42-93843
B-29A-5-BN	42-93844/42-93873
B-29A-10-BN	42-93874/42-93923
B-29A-15-BN	42-93924/42-93973
B-29A-20-BN	42-93974/42-94023
B-29A-25-BN	42-94024/42-94073
B-29A-30-BN	42-94074/42-94123
B-29-35-MO	44-27259/44-27325
B-29-40-MO	44-27326/44-27358
B-29A-35-BN	44-61510/44-61609
B-29A-40-BN	44-61610/44-61709
B-19A-45-BN	44-61710/44-61806
B-29A-50-BN	44-61810/44-61909
B-29A-55-BN	44-61910/44-62009
B-29A-60-BN	44-62010/44-62109
B-29A-65-BN	44-62110/44-62209
B-29A-70-BN	44-62210/44-62309
B-29A-75-BN	44-62310/44-62328
B-29-55-BW	44-69655/44-69704
B-29-60-BW	44-69705/44-69804
B-29-65-BW	44-69805/44-69904
B-29-70-BW	44-69905/44-70004
B-29-75-BW	44-70005/44-70104
B-29-80-BW	44-70105/44-70154
B-29B-40-BA	44-83890/44-83893
B-29-40-BA	44-83894
B-29B-40-BA	44-83895
B-29B-45-BA	44-83896/44-83899
B-29-45-BA	44-83900
B-29B-45-BA	44-83901/44-83903
B-29-45-BA	44-83904
B-29B-45-BA	44-83905/44-83907
B-29-45-BA	44-83908
B-29B-45-BA	44-83909/44-83910
B-29-45-BA	44-83911
B-29B-45-BA	44-83912/44-83913
B-29-45-BA	44-83914

BLOCK	SERIAL
B-29B-45-BA	44-83915/44-83916
B-29-45-BA	44-83917
B-29B-45-BA	44-83918/44-83919
B-29-45-BA	44-83920
B-29B-45-BA	44-83921/44-83922
B-29-45-BA	44-83923
B-29B-45-BA	44-83924/44-83925
NOTE 1	44-83926/44-83943
NOTE 2	44-83944/44-83958
B-29B-45-BA	44-83959
B-29-45-BA	44-83960
B-29B-45-BA	44-83961
B-29-45-BA	44-83962
NOTE 3	44-83963/44-84008
NOTE 4	44-84009/44-84056
NOTE 5	44-84057/44-84103
NOTE 6	44-84104/44-84152

BLOCK	SERIAL
B-29B-65-BA	44-84155
B-29-65-BA	44-84156
B-29-40-MO	44-86242/44-86276
B-29-45-MO	44-86277/44-86315
B-29-50-MO	44-86316/44-86370
B-29-55-MO	44-86371/44-86425
B-29-60-MO	44-86426/44-86472
B-29-80-BW	44-87584/44-87633
B-29-85-BW	44-87634/44-87683
B-29-86-BW	44-87684/44-87733
B-29-90-BW	44-87734/44-87783
	45-21693/45-21742
B-29-95-BW	45-21758/45-21792
	45-21813/45-21842
B-29-97-BW	45-21743/45-21757
B-29-96-BW	45-21793/45-21812
B-29-100-BW	45-21843/45-21872

NOTES:

1 B-29-45-BA even S/N and B-29B-45-BA odd S/N
2 B-29-45-BA odd S/N and B-29B-45-BA even S/N
3 B-29B-50-BA odd S/N and B-29-50-BA even S/N
4 B-29B-55-BA odd S/N and B-29-55-BA even S/N
5 B-29B-60-BA odd S/N and B-29-60-BA even S/N
6 B-29B-65-BA odd S/N and B-29-65-BA even S/N

As a matter of interest it should be noted that the requirements for the B-29 became so great that a fifth manufacturer was contracted with to produce an additional 200 aircraft. The North American version would have been designated as B-29-NA and carried the serial numbers 42-14502/14701. This order was cancelled before production began.

B-29 PRODUCTION SUMMARY

TYPE	NO. BUILT	PLANT
XB-29-BO	3	Boeing-Seattle
YB-29-BW	14	Boeing-Wichita
B-29-BW	1,630	Boeing-Wichita
B-29-BA	357	Bell-Atlanta
B-29-MO	531	Martin-Omaha
B-29A-BN	1,119	Boeing-Renton
B-29B-BA	311	Bell-Atlanta
	3,965 TOTAL	

DIMENSIONS

Actual

DIMENSION	AIRCRAFT				
	XB-29	YB-29	B-29	B-29A	B-29B
Wing Span (ft. in.)	141′ 2.76″	141′ 2.76″	141′ 2.76″	142′ 2.76″	141′ 2.76″
Wing Root Chord (ft. in.)	17′ 0.00″	17′ 0.00″	17′ 0.00″	17′ 0.00″	17′ 0.00″
Wing Tip Chord (ft. in.)	7′ 5.00″	7′ 5.00″	7′ 5.00″	7′ 5.00″	7′ 5.00″
Wing Area (sq. ft.)	1,736	1,736	1,736	1,739	1,736
Aileron Span (ft. in.)	25′ 10.00″	25′ 10.00″	25′ 10.00″	25′ 10.00″	25′10.00″
Flap Span (ft. in.)	37′ 8.43″	37′ 8.43″	37′ 8.43″	37′ 8.43″	37′ 8.43″
Length (ft. in.)	98′ 1.92″	99′ 0.00″	99′ 0.00″	99′ 0.00″	99′ 0.00″
Height (ft. in.)	27′ 9.00″	27′ 9.00″	27′ 9.00″	27′ 9.00″	27′ 9.00″
Rudder Height (ft. in.)	14′ 7.25″	12′ 0.18″	12′ 0.18″	12′ 0.18″	12′ 0.18″
Horizontal Stabilizer Span (ft. in.)	43′ 0.00″	43′ 0.00″	43′ 0.00″	43′ 0.00″	43′ 0.00″
Horizontal Stabilizer Root Chord (ft. in.)	11′ 2.40″	11′ 2.40″	11′ 2.40″	11′ 2.40″	11′ 2.40″
Vertical Fin Area (sq. ft.)	237.8	237.8	237.8	238.8	237.8
Horizontal Tail Area (sq. ft.)	333.0	333.0	333.0	333.0	333.0
MLG Track (ft. in.)	28′ 5.60″	28′ 5.60″	28′ 5.60″	28′ 5.60″	28′ 5.60″
MLG Tire Diameter (in.)	56.00″	56.00″	56.00″	56.00″	56.00″
NLG Tire Diameter (in.)	36.00″	36.00″	36.00″	36.00″	36.00″
Propeller Diameter (ft. in.)	17′ 0.00″	17′ 0.00″	16′ 7.00″	16′ 7.00″	16′ 7.00″

1/72nd Scale in Inches

DIMENSION	AIRCRAFT				
	XB-29	YB-29	B-29	B-29A	B-29B
Wing Span	23.54	23.54	23.54	23.71	23.54
Wing Root Chord	2.83	2.83	2.83	2.83	2.83
Wing Tip Chord	1.24	1.24	1.24	1.24	1.24
Aileron Span	4.30	4.30	4.30	4.30	4.30
Flap Span	6.28	6.28	6.28	6.28	6.28
Length	16.36	16.50	16.50	16.50	16.50
Height	4.63	4.63	4.63	4.63	4.63
Rudder Height	2.43	2.00	2.00	2.00	2.00
Horizontal Stabilizer Span	7.17	7.17	7.17	7.17	7.17
Horizontal Stabilizer Root Chord	1.87	1.87	1.87	1.87	1.87
MLG Track	7.74	4.74	4.74	4.74	4.74
MLG Tire Diameter	0.78	0.78	0.78	0.78	0.78
NLG Tire Diameter	0.50	0.50	0.50	0.50	0.50
Propeller Diameter	2.83	2.83	2.76	2.76	2.76

1/48th Scale in Inches

DIMENSION	AIRCRAFT				
	XB-29	YB-29	B-29	B-29A	B-29B
Wing Span	35.31	35.31	35.31	35.56	35.31
Wing Root Chord	4.25	4.25	4.25	4.25	4.25
Wing Tip Chord	1.85	1.85	1.85	1.85	1.85
Aileron Span	6.45	6.45	6.45	6.45	6.45
Flap Span	9.42	9.42	9.42	9.42	9.42
Length	24.54	24.75	24.75	24.75	24.75
Height	6.94	6.94	6.94	6.94	6.94
Rudder Height	3.65	3.00	3.00	3.00	3.00
Horizontal Stabilizer Span	10.75	10.75	10.75	10.75	10.75
Horizontal stabilizer Root Chord	2.80	2.80	2.80	2.80	2.80
MLG Track	7.12	7.12	7.12	7.12	7.12
MLG Tire Diameter	1.17	1.17	1.17	1.17	1.17
NLG Tire Diameter	0.75	0.75	0.75	0.75	0.75
Propeller Diameter	4.25	4.25	4.15	4.15	4.15

MODELER'S SECTION

PRODUCT REVIEW POLICY. In each of our publications we will try to review kits and decals that are available to the scale modeler. We hope to be able to review every currently available kit that is useable by the scale modeler. Kits produced in the past that are no longer generally available, and those more intended to be toys than accurate scale models will not usually be covered. Additionally, we do not intend to give a complete step-by-step, correction-by-correction account of how to build each kit. Instead we intend to give a brief description of what is available to the modeler, and point out some of the good and not-so-good points of each kit or product. In this way we hope to give an overall picture of what the modeler has readily available for his use in building the particular aircraft involved.

1/144TH SCALE KIT

1/144th Scale Crown Kit No. 483/Revell Kit No. 1049

A total of 57 silver and 7 clear pieces comprise this compact kit. The molding is crisp, but the turrets appear a bit too rounded. The vertical fin shape was apparently taken from the WW-II-vintage Wylam drawing which was in error due presumably to security reasons. The twin-row, 18-cylinder engines have been reasonably simulated, although the gearbox case should have been made in a bullet-shape. On the front face of the cowlings, the relative sizes of the main air inlet and the oil cooler inlet are misproportioned. Either propellers or prop hubs may be installed to simulate engine operation. Where space is of concern, this 11.75-inch wing span will fit in nicely.

Crown/Revell 1/144th scale B-29. ***(Lloyd)***

1/120TH SCALE KIT

1/120 Scale Revell Kit No. 4301

This venerable kit shows its age with the heavy rivet pattern, but its outline is quite accurate. For the front end crew there is a floor with instrument panels, an asile stand, and three crewmen. The kit does not offer landing gear, but the simple stand is adequate. Mounting this model on a wooden base would be ideal for an ex-B-29er. In the black-belly color scheme the model is quite attractive. The completed model has a 14 inch wing span.

Revell 1/120th scale model on a stand. ***(Lloyd)***

1/72ND SCALE KIT

1/72 Scale Airfix Kit No. 07001-4/USAirfix Kit No. 5102/MPC Kit No. 3001-07 & Kit No. 8-14501

After passing through so many. molding, this ancient kit is still holding up. There is a plenthora of parts requiring a great deal of time and effort to assemble. Over 200 pieces are included. Probably the most difficult task is to join the two fuselage halves while retaining the alignment of the nose gear strut, floors and bulkheads, four turrets, and the rudder.

Much interior detail has been provided in the kit to include a fairly complete flight deck and waist compartment. The four bomb bay doors may be built in the open position to reveal a bay with a pair of pressure bulkheads, a communications tunnel, and eight bomb racks. Up to 16 500-pound bombs may be hung on the bomb racks. Experience has shown that it is best to build the kit with the bomb bay doors in the open position because of the poor fit, otherwise much filling and sanding is required if the doors are to be closed. Five pieces comprise each turret. Optional twin and four-gun mounts are provided for the top forward turret. A tail gun position has twin .50 caliber guns with an optional 20 mm cannon.

A tail skid and actuator are included. The crew aft entry door may be left open and the access ladder

USAirfix B-29 built as "Dina Might." ***(Lloyd)***

Airfix 1/72nd scale B-29 ***(Lloyd)***

installed. Mounting provisions for the ECM gear found on earlier aircraft have been molded into the fuselage nose and should be sanded out if not required on the specific aircraft being modeled. The APU compartment hatch located on the aft left portion of the fuselage is too long, and no belly radar is provided.

The landing gear is quite complete. A total of seven pieces comprise the nose gear while eight pieces make up each main gear. If installed per the instructions, the main gear will be splayed because the kit design did not take the wing dihedral into account. Experience has shown that it is best to install the main gear late in the assembly process, clip off one of the trunnion pivot lugs, and align the strut so that all main wheels are in the correct plane.

The duplication of the R-3350 engines is quite good. Detailing of the huge Hamilton Standard hydromatic propellers is impressive. When the props and engines are coupled with the cowlings, a rather impressive power package results. Eight individual engine exhausts are provided, but care must be taken to ensure the proper location of these components.

Over the years numerous markings have been offered with the various issues of this kit. The last USAirfix issue contained markings for "Dina Might." MPC is reissuing the kit with the 6th Bomb Group's "Jolly Roger" markings.

This kit with its 23.3-inch wing span is worth the effort to build.

1/48TH SCALE KIT

1/48th Scale Monogram Kit No. 5700

From start to finish, this kit is impressive in the Monogram tradition. Firstly, the kit packaging is sturdy to minimize breakage. The instructions are clear and straight forward, and since the kit can be built into alternative versions, the instructions clearly point out the differences.

The kit is an interior detailer's delight. From the flight deck to the tail gunner's position, interior components abound. The only drawback is that there is no clear side so that the modeler can display his detailing handiwork. One magazine article showed the kit built with sections of the fuselage cutaway so that the interior could be viewed on the completed model. This is not a bad idea if the interior is well-detailed by the modeler.

The flight deck contains all of the major components: panels, crew equipment, controls, and wire bundles for a standard B-29. A fully detailed nose wheel well is provided. The interior structure of the bomb bay with pressure bulkheads, communications tunnel, bomb racks, and structure are included. An aft crew compartment complete with gunners' seats, bulkheads, and crew bunks are in the kit. In the tail is a finely detailed tail skid and gunner's position. A highly detailed set of main landing gear wheel wells are provided. A rack of oxygen bottles is provided for installation between the bomb bays. Bomb bay doors with the later pneumatic actuators are likewise included. The bomb bay loads include Fat Man and Little Boy atomic bombs and a pair of fuel tanks. A late model AN/APQ-13 belly radar antenna fairing is also provided. Other antennas include the ADF football, RC-103 blind landing horseshoe, and mast antennas.

Monogram 1/48th scale kit with Scalemaster decals for "Monsoon Goon" ***(Lloyd)***

Monogram B-29 kit in "Thumper" markings. ***(Monogram)***

The wings are sturdy, and a pair of realistic spars are included to afford added strength for the installation of the structure visible within the bomb bays.

Barrel-like turret bodies are provided for insertion into the fuselage. Turret covers with twin and four gun installations fit nicely on the turret bodies. The tail turret has a canvas-like boot with a pair of .50 caliber machine guns and a 20 mm cannon. A set of turret-hole plugs are provided for the atomic bombers.

Nicely detailed cowls are included, and the cowl flaps are molded in the closed position. The engine is molded with a full front cylinder row, ignition harness horsecollar, reduction gear case, front oil sump, and distributors. Unfortunately only a semblance of the aft cylinder row is molded between the front cylinder row and the firewall. On a kit of this size a fully detailed engine would have been a most desirable feature. The propellers in the kit are of the lesser used Curtiss electric variety. They are well detailed. To make them into the more predominately used Hamilton Standard hydromatic propellers would require considerable reshaping of each blade to remove the cuffs and straighten the leading and trailing edges. In addition, the propeller hub would have to be recontoured.

A number of fine clear parts are provided. Even the wing tip navigation light lenses are in the kit as separate clear parts.

For those wishing to make a diorama, four figures and a bomb dolly are provided. In addition, there is an excellent set of full-color instructions by noted modeler Shep Paine.

We highly recommend this kit.

Monogram kit interior cockpit details. This kit has extensive interior detailing. ***(Lloyd)***

Monogram kit interior waist and tail position details. ***(Lloyd)***

HAMILTON STANDARD NON-CUFFED CONVERSION PROPELLERS

299 Models of Seattle, Washington has released a conversion kit, number 002, which contains injection molded conversion propellers for the Monogram kit in 1/48th scale. These propellers are the Hamilton Standard non-cuffed propellers and hubs, and they are designed to replace the cuffed Curtiss electric propellers provided in the kit. To order this kit send $3.00 plus 40¢ postage to, The Triple Alliance, 10328 Main Street, Bellevue, Washington 98004.

1/72nd Scale Drawings

AN/APQ-7 EAGLE RADAR

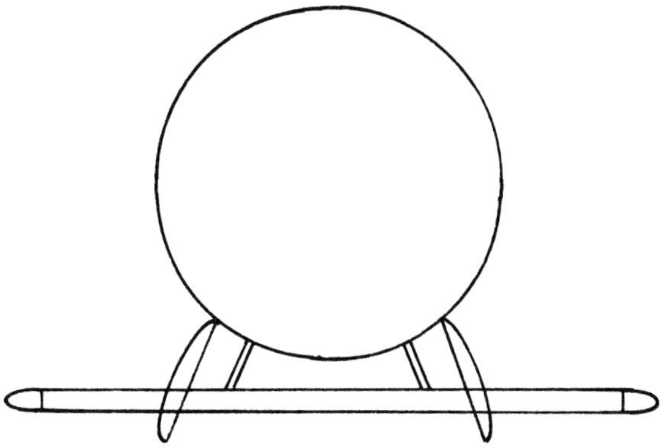

FRONT VIEW

BOTTOM VIEW

AN/APG-15 GUN LAYING RADAR

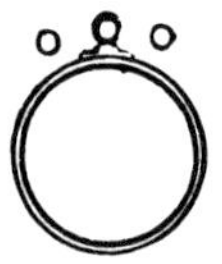

REAR VIEW

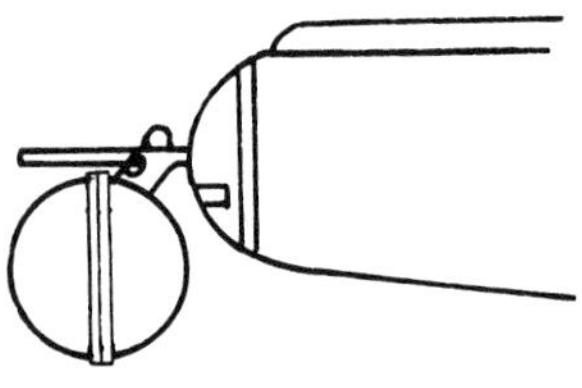

SIDE VIEW

Shown here are 1/72nd scale drawings of the AN/APQ-7 Eagle Radar and the AN/APG-15 Gun Laying radar for modelers that might want to convert a model of a B-29 to a B-29B. In 1/48th scale, the AN/APQ-7 Eagle Radar would be 4.5 inches wide at the centerline, and would have a chord of .65 inches. The AN/APQ-15 would have a diameter of .72 inches.

Airfix B-29 converted to a B-29B with an AN/APQ-7 Eagle radar and an AN/APG-15 gun laying radar.(Lloyd)

DECALS

1/144th SCALE

NAME	S/N	TYPE	AF	WG	GP	SQ	TAIL CODE	A/C NO.	DECAL SOURCE
Dina Might	42-65286	B-29-25-MO	21	313	504	421	Circle E (1)	29 (1)	Crown Kit 483, Revell Kit 1049
-	-	-	21	314	29	-	Box O	6	Crown Kit 483, Revell Kit 1049
-	-	-	21	315	331	-	Diamond L	3	Crown Kit 483, Revell Kit 1049
-	-	-	21	73	493	-	A	23	Crown Kit 483, Revell Kit 1049

1/120th SCALE

NAME	S/N	TYPE	AF	WG	GP	SQ	TAIL CODE	A/C NO.	DECAL SOURCE
-	-	-	21	58	444	678	Triangle N	30	Revell Kit 4301

1/72nd SCALE

NAME	S/N	TYPE	AF	WG	GP	SQ	TAIL CODE	A/C NO.	DECAL SOURCE
Battlin' Betty III	44-79772	B-29-60-BW	21	73	498	875	T Square	48	MPC Kit 2-0551
Belle Ringer	42-63464	B-29-20-BA	20	58	468	794	Yellow Stripes		ESCI Sheet 9 (2)
Bockscar	44-27279	B-29-35-MO	21	313	509	373	Triangle N	77	ESCI Sheet 9 (3)
							or		Microscale Sheet 72-151 (7)
							Circle Arrow		MPC Kit 3001-07
Coral Queen	42-24615	B-29-41-BW	21	73	497	869	A Square	8	Microscale Sheet 72-151 (7)
Cream of the Crop	44-61657	B-29A-40-BN		(8)	19	30	Keystone Cop	-	Fowler Sheet 7203 (4)
Dina Might	42-65286	B-29-25-MO	21	313	504	421	Circle E (1)	29 (1)	ESCI Sheet 9
							Circle E	29	USAirfix Kit 5102
Dragon Lady	44-61835	B-29A-50-BN		(8)	19	28	Indian Head	-	Fowler Sheet 7203
Eddie Allen	42-24597	B-29-40-BW	20	58	40	45	Yellow Stripes	-	Airfix Kit 07001-4
Enola Gay	44-86292	B-29-45-MO	21	313	509	373	Circle R	82	ABT Sheet 15
							Circle R	82	MPC Kit 3001-07
Honshu Hawk	42-63444	B-29-40-BW	21	73	498	875	T Square	45	MPC Kit 3001-07
Jolly Roger	-	-	21	313	6	-	Circle R		MPC Kit 8-14501
Joltin' Josie	42-24624	B-29-40-BW	21	73	498	873	T Square	5	Airfix Kit 07001-4
Lady Eve II	42-24663	B-29-40-BW	21	73	498	875	T Square	43	ESCI Sheet 9
Never Hoppen	44-61562	B-29A-35-BN		(8)	19	28	Indian Head	-	Fowler Sheet 7203
Nip on Nees	44-62261	B-29A-70-BN		(8)	98		Box H	-	Microscale Sheet 72-356
(Pirates Head)	42-24536	B-29-35-BW	21	313	6	24	Circle R	4	Microscale Sheet 72-151 (7)
So Tired, Seven to Seven	44-61727	RB-29A-45-BN	15			91	Circle X	-	Microscale Sheet 72-356
South Sea Sinner	-	-		(8)	19	28	Box M (5)	-	ESCI Sheet 9
Top of the Mark	-	-		(8)			Box M (5)	-	ESCI Sheet 9
Yokohama Yo-Yo	42-24621	F-13A-40-BW	21	73	-	3	F	-	IPMS 1975 Special Sheet

1/48th SCALE

NAME	S/N	TYPE	AF	WG	GP	SQ	TAIL CODE	A/C NO.	DECAL SOURCE
Battlin' Betty III	42-96772	B-29-60-BW	21	73	498	875	T	41	Microscale Sheet 48-45
The Great Artiste	42-27353	B-29-40-MO	21	313	509	393	Circle Arrow	89	Microscale Sheet 48-44
Joltin' Josie	42-24614	B-29-40-BW	21	73	498	873	T Square	5	Microscale Sheet 48-45
Monsoon Goon	42-93828	B-29A-1-BN	20	58	468	794	Yellow Stripe	-	Scalemaster Sheet
Next Objective	44-27299	B-29-35-MO	21	313	509	393	Triangle N	86	Microscale Sheet 48-44
Nip On Nees	44-62261	B-29A-70-BN		(8)	98		Box H	-	Microscale Sheet 48-130
Straight Flush	44-27301	B-29-35-MO	21	313	509	393	Triangle N	85	Microscale Sheet 48-44
Strange Cargo	44-27300	B-29-35-MO	21	313	509	393	Circle Arrow	73	Microscale Sheet 48-44
Thumper (6)	42-24623	B-29-40-BW	21	73	497	870	A	21	Monogram Kit
Thunderbird	42-63454	B-29-20-BA	21	58	462	768	X	3	Microscale Sheet 48-45

(1) Markings not included on decal sheet
(2) Only nose art is provided
(3) Background disc should be yellow not blue
(4) Comes with separate overlay to censor nose art
(5) Box M was WW II tail code for 19th BG and not used in Korea for which the markings are provided
(6) Name is provided for one side only
(7) Microscale Sheet 72-151 also has PW SUPPLIES markings included
(8) Far East Bomber Command (FEAF BC) Korea War

REFERENCE LISTING

Note: Listed here are references on the B-29 Superfortress that should prove helpful in providing information and photographs of a different nature and format than what is presented in this publication. There are many fine references on the B-29 Superfortress and they all cannot be listed here. The fact that a given reference is not included in this list is not intended to reflect unfavorably on that reference.

1. Anderton, D.A., B-29 Superfortress at War, Chas. Scribner's, N.Y., 1978.
2. Anderton, D.A., The Story of the U.S. Air Force, Crescent, N.Y., 1981.
3. Arnold, H.H., Global Mission, Harper, N.Y., 1949.
4. Berger, C., The B-29 Superfortress, Ballantine, N.Y., 1976.
5. Birdsall, S., B-29 Superfortress in Action, Squadron/Signal, Carrolton, TX., 1977.
6. Birdsall, S., Saga of the Superfortress, Doubleday, N.Y., 1980.
7. Birdsall, S., Superfortress: The Boeing B-29, Squadron/Signal, Carrolton, TX., 1980.
8. Bowers, P.M., Boeing Aircraft Since 1916, Putnam, London, 1966.
9. Caidin, M., Air Force - A Pictorial History of American Airpower, Rinehart, N.Y., 1957.
10. Chinook, F.W., Nagasaki: The Forgotten Bomb, World, N.Y., 1969.
11. Collison, T., The Superfortress is Born, Duell, Sloan, & Pearce, N.Y., 1945.
12. Craven, W.F. & Cate, J.L., The Army Air Forces in World War II, Univ. of Chicago Press, Chicago, 1948.
13. Carter, K.C., & Mueller, R., The Army Air Forces in World War II - Combat Chronology 1941-1945, U.S. Government Printing Office, Washington, D.C., 1973.
14. Fahey, J.C., U.S. Army Aircraft 1909-1946, Ships and Aircraft, N.Y., 1946.
15. Fahey, J.C., USAF Aircraft 1947-1956, Ships and Aircraft, Falls Church, VA, 1956.
16. Goldberg, A., A History of the United States Air Force 1907-1957, D. van Nostrand, N.J., 1958.
17. Green, W., Famous Bombers of the Second World War, Vol. 2, Hanover House, N.Y., 1960.
18. Gurney, E., Journey of the Giants, Coward-McCann, N.Y., 1961.
19. Jablonski, E., Airwar, Vol. 2, Doubleday, N.Y., 1971.
20. Jane's All the World's Aircraft, MacMillian, N.Y., 1945-1951.
21. Johnsen, F.A., The B-29 Book, Bomber Books, Tacoma, WA, 1978.
22. Jones, L.S., U.S. Bombers, B-1 - B-70, Aero Publishers, Fallbrook, CA, 1962.
23. Jones, L.S., U.S. Bombers, Army and Air Force, Aero Publishers, Fallbrook, CA., 1980.
24. Mason, H.M., Jr., The United States Air Force: A Turbulent History, Mason/Charter, N.Y., 1976.
25. Mayborn, M., The Boeing B-29 Superfortress, Vol. 101, Profile Publications, Surrey, England, 1966.
26. Morrison, W.H., Hellbirds: The Story of the B-29 in Combat, Zenger, Wash., D.C., 1979.
27. Morrison, W.H., Point of No Return: The Story of the 20th Air Force, Time Books, N.Y., 1979.
28. LeMay, C.E., & Kanton, M., Mission with LeMay, Doubleday, N.Y., 1965.
29. Pimlott, J., B-29 Superfortress, Bison Books, London/K-Mart, Troy, MI, 1980.
30. Rust, K., Twentieth Air Force Story, Historical Aviation Album, Temple City, CA., 1979.
31. Siefring, T.A., U.S. Air Force in World War II, Chartwell Books, N.Y., 1977.
32. Simon & Schuster Encyclopedia of World War II, Simon & Schuster, N.Y., 1978.
33. Sinclair, W.B., The Big Brothers: The Story of the B-29, Naylor Press, San Antonio, TX., 1972.
34. Snyder, E.A., General LeMay's Circus: A Navigator's Story of the 20th Air Force in World War II, Exposition Press, N.Y., 1955.
35. Sunderman, J.F., World War II in the Air - The Pacific, Franklin Watts, N.Y., 1962.
36. Swanborough, G., & Bowers, P.M., United States Military Aircraft Since 1909, Putnam, London, 1963.
37. Swanborough, G., & Bowers, P.M., United States Navy Aircraft Since 1911, Putnam, London, 1968 & 1976.
38. The Aircraft Year Book, Lancair, N.Y., 1945 thru 1951.
39. Thetford, O., Aircraft of the Royal Air Force Since 1918, Putnam, London, 1962.
40. Thomas, G., & Witts, M.M., Enola Gay, Stein & Day, 1977.
41. Wagner, R., American Combat Planes, Hanover House, Garden City, N.Y., 1960.